John Fotheringham,

A CODE OF ETHICS
FOR SOCIAL WORK

Pamela Fotheringham.

A CODE OF ETHICS FOR SOCIAL WORK
The second step

edited by
David Watson
in association with the
British Association of Social Workers

foreword by
John Cypher
General Secretary

BASW

Routledge & Kegan Paul
London, Boston, Melbourne and Henley

First pubished in 1985
by Routledge & Kegan Paul plc,

14 Leicester Square,
London WC2H 7PH, England,

9 Park Street, Boston, Mass. 02108, USA,

464 St Kilda Road, Melbourne,
Victoria 3004, Australia and

Broadway House, Newtown Road,
Henley-on-Thames, Oxon RG9 1EN, England

Set in Sabon 10/12 pt
by Hope Services, Abingdon
and printed in Great Britain
by T.J. Press (Padstow) Ltd,
Padstow, Cornwall

Library of Congress Cataloging in Publication Data

A Code of ethics for social work.
Bibliography: p.
Includes index.
1. Social workers – Professional ethics – Great Britain
– Addresses, essays, lectures.   2. Social service –
Great Britain – Moral and ethical aspects – Addresses,
essays, lectures.   I. Watson, David, 1946–
II. British Association of Social Workers.
HV243.C63   1985   174'.9362'0941   84–18053

British Library CIP Data available

ISBN 0–7102–0454–X (p)

ISBN 0–7102–0611–9 (c)

We shall not cease from exploration
And the end of all our exploring
Will be to arrive where we started
And know the place for the first time

T. S. Eliot, *Four Quartets: Little Gidding*,
London, Faber & Faber, 1944, V, lines 239–42.

Contents

viii Contents

Foreword

John Cypher
General Secretary, British Association of Social Workers

The publication of this book coincides with the tenth anniversary of the adoption by the British Association of Social Workers of a Code of Ethics. It was at the Edinburgh Annual General Meeting in 1975 that the Code was debated and endorsed and all persons joining BASW are required to give an undertaking that they have read, and will abide by, the Code.

Now ten years on the opportunity is presented to analyse in detail aspects of the Code and to provide a new opportunity to bring to centre stage in professional debate such questions as whether or not a Code of Ethics for social workers is useful, and more particularly, what changes, if any, might be needed to the BASW Code? David Watson in his introductory essay observes that a Code of Ethics is useful if it makes explicit 'the ends and means to which practitioners are committed'. Readers of this book are invited to form their own view about the BASW Code and, if they so choose, to contact me with their reactions. These will be given serious consideration in discussions within the Association about recasting or representing the Code of Ethics.

In devising and publishing a Code of Ethics BASW has taken the view that there is merit in providing guidance to its members on how to approach judgments about professional intervention, given that there are moral dilemmas intrinsic to much social work practice. The Code may also be relevant in calling to account members who are alleged to have acted unprofessionally. But can it be that the Code is either so little known or of such limited value that it does not require the serious consideration to which it is subject in this book? Surprisingly, there is no reference to the BASW Code in the report of the Barclay Committee published under the title *Social Workers: Their Role and Tasks* (Barclay, 1982). Although describing their work as an attempt to offer 'such a clarification as we could encompass of exceedingly complex questions' no reference is made to the utility of any Code of Ethics for social workers. Perhaps this is unsurprising given that the Barclay Committee chose to locate the too brief discussion of values, methods, skills and knowledge within that section of their report called 'context'. In reality moral concerns are of the essence of social work practice and the fact that most social workers in the United Kingdom are employees of local authorities does not minimise the importance of receiving guidance about, and undertaking, ethical practice.

Of course no Code of Ethics can or should serve as a set of rules prescribing for social workers how they should conduct themselves in helping and caring for strangers, but the BASW Code's general principles are intended to give some guidance about approaching those recurring situations in practice raising ethical concerns. For example: What are this child's best interests? Should this person's wish to die be respected? In what circumstances should this information given in confidence be shared with others? Can involvement in a trade union dispute be reconciled with professional responsibilities to clients?

For members of BASW the Code is not the last word in dealing with moral issues of these kinds. From time to time more specific guidance is produced drawing on the Code's principles of practice. Recent examples of further guidance concern the social worker's role in the decision making about the welfare of newly born severely handicapped infants (BASW, 1982); the pursuit of effective and ethical case recording (BASW, 1983a) detailing the principles of an ethical records system for social work agencies (so limiting to what is necessary the exercise of state power over the individual – which is how record keeping can be seen); the social worker's relationship with employing agencies (BASW, 1983b) taking account both of professional obligations and requirements of a social worker as employee; and social work practice with children in care (BASW, 1983c), which recognises the centrality of the child's best interest having regard to fundamental questions of civil liberties and differing philosophies concerning the role of the family.

In the view of some, a Code of Ethics adopted by a professional occupation is to be seen as not so much a guide to the conduct required of members of that profession, but having more to do with professional aggrandisement. In their *Dictionary of Social Welfare* (an aid in thinking and talking about welfare) Timms and Timms (1982, pp. 34–5) speak of the BASW Code saying 'such codification enhances professional status'. If this is a consequence, in BASW's case it is essentially a by-product for unequivocally the Association has set its sights on moving social work towards a partnership in practice in which there is shared working between social work and clients. At the very same meeting in 1975 at which the Association approved a Code of Ethics, an address was given by Bill Jordan which inspired a range of work culminating in the major policy statement of 1980 *Clients are Fellow Citizens* (BASW, 1980). In his introduction to that document Patrick Phelan, the then BASW Chairman, observes that 'sharing in social work maintains for our clients their complete citizenship and serves to make explicit the aims of social work practice and the values on which we base it'. By describing and discussing how in the practice of social work the client is a full and fellow citizen, the document in question embraces and operationalises the ideals contained in the Code of Ethics.

At its 1982 Annual General Meeting BASW took stock of where social work is in moving along a continuum from professionalism beyond participation and on to partnership. To assist in that stock-taking Professor Paul Wilding challenged social work and indeed all professions to forge a new relationship based on partnership: between professional and client, professional and society and between professionals and other professionals. (Wilding, 1982a; Wilding 1982b). In the case of the profession of social work BASW is responding to Wilding's challenge. BASW's Code of Ethics, ten years on, is still an important corner stone in building this partnership and in the various guidance documents (some of which are mentioned above) derived from the Code, assistance is given to help members in achieving a fuller expression of partnership on all fronts.

But what befalls those BASW members who breach the Association's Code? Timms and Timms comment (1982), 'it has been said that as far as social work is concerned misconduct is undefinable' (here misconduct is seen as behaviour that may be a violation of the Code). BASW has been giving attention to this too and in a recent statement (BASW, 1983d) the Association's Disciplinary Board has viewed professional misconduct as 'an act or omission (whether or not it is unlawful) which is actually or potentially likely to be substantially (a) harmful to clients, colleagues or members of public; or (b) prejudicial to the development or standing of social work practice; or (c) contrary to the Code of Ethics.'

It is noted that as the Code is a statement of principles, departure from it may not amount to conduct requiring the use of the disciplinary procedures. Examples of conduct which may amount to professional misconduct are set out, and their origin clearly traced to the Code's principles of practice. Under these new provisions members of BASW referred for alleged professional misconduct will be advised of the complaint; this and the member's reaction (if any) will then be considered by an investigating committee which is independent of the Disciplinary Board; and this committee will determine whether or not the complaint is in respect of professional misconduct as defined by BASW. If it is, the member will be summoned to a meeting of the Board which has a range of sanctions available, including expulsion from membership. In viewing the Code of Ethics and the disciplinary procedures as complementary parts of the system for ensuring the discharge by BASW members of their professional obligations, the Association is able to respond to the concern of Timms and Timms that social workers and clients 'are often in vulnerable "private" situations which demand more than administrative appeal or complaint' (1982).

It is not enough that measures of this kind intended to ensure ethical practice should be confined only to members of BASW and be of benefit only to clients served by them. The powerlessness of many of the clients of social workers and the significance of social workers' decisions for the individual's welfare require provisions which will ensure ethical practice by all in social work. For this reason BASW favours the establishment of a general social work council as the essential next step in procuring real partnership in practice.

Notes on contributors

DAVID WATSON is a lecturer in Social Administration at the University of Bristol. His publications in the field of philosophy and public policy include *Caring for Strangers*, 1980. He was a member of Strathclyde Children's Panel.

RUTH WILKES is honorary lecturer in Social Administration at the University of Birmingham. She has considerable experience as a practitioner, manager, researcher and teacher, particularly in health care. Her publications include *Social Work with Undervalued Groups*, 1981.

NEIL LEIGHTON is an Engineering graduate; he has worked in probation, child care, family casework and social services over a period of twenty-five years. His publications include joint authorship of *Rights and Responsibilities*, 1982.

GAVIN FAIRBAIRN is Teacher-in-charge of a child psychiatric unit in Oldham and has previous experience of both field and residential social work.

MALCOLM PAYNE is Chief Executive to the Liverpool Council for Voluntary Service. He previously worked as a probation and after-care officer, social worker, senior social worker and area officer in various social services departments, and as a lecturer in social work at Bristol University. He was for several years on BASW's Education and Training, and Professional Practice Committees, and its Ethics and Ethical Issues Advisory Panel. He is the author of two books, *Power, Authority and Responsibility in Social Services*, 1979, and *Working in Teams*, 1982.

HUW RICHARDS is Director of LINK: Glasgow Association for Mental Health. He was educated at Keble College, Oxford and qualified as a social worker at Glasgow University. He has worked in community work and various fields of mental health.

JOHN R. HUDSON came into social work through voluntary work and much of his experience was gained in various assessment centres and their predecessors. In 1976 he was appointed Officer in Charge of a home for 16–18-year-olds and in 1978 moved to Huddersfield Polytechnic to become responsible for the residential work specialism of the CQSW course. From 1974–9 he was a member of BASW's Education and Training Committee and since 1979 has been a member, appointed by BASW, of the Central Council for Education and Training in Social Work. He was also a regular contributor for six years to the 'In residence' column of *Social Work Today*.

JOAN K. SUTHERLAND is a former General Practitioner with over forty years' experience. She has long been concerned with general issues raised by medical practice, and is a member of the Central Ethical Committee of the British Medical Association, and the Committee on Doctors and Social Workers.

Acknowledgments

A number of people have contributed support in a variety of ways. I should particularly like to thank John Cypher and Patrick Phelan for encouragement and comment, Dominga de la Cruz, Sue Richards and Kiran Chauhan for administration and typing, Ann Friend and Patrick Oakley for contributions to our preliminary workshop, and Noel Timms and Gwynn Davis for supportive, and piercing, comment on my own contributions. I should like to thank BASW for permission to reproduce *A Code of Ethics for Social Work*.

David Watson

A Code of Ethics for Social Work

The Code which follows was adopted by BASW at the Annual General Meeting, Edinburgh, 1975. All members of the Association are required to uphold the Code.

Objectives

1 Social work is a professional activity. Implicit in its practice are ethical principles which prescribe the professional responsibility of the social worker. The primary objective of the Code of Ethics is to make these implicit principles explicit for the protection of clients.

Foreword

2 Membership of any profession entails certain obligations beyond those of the ordinary citizen. A profession's code of ethics sets down, in general terms, those special obligations, and specifies particular duties which follow from them.

3 Members of a profession have obligations to their clients, to their employers, to each other, to colleagues in other disciplines and to society.

4 In order to carry out these obligations, the professional has complementary rights which must be respected for him to work effectively.

5 Any professional association has the duty to secure, as far as possible that its members discharge their professional obligations; and that members are afforded in full necessary professional rights.

2 A Code of Ethics for Social Work

Statement of principles

6 Basic to the profession of social work is the recognition of the value and dignity of every human being, irrespective of origin, status, sex, sexual orientation, age, belief or contribution to society. The profession accepts a responsibility to encourage and facilitate the self-realisation of the individual person with due regard for the interest of others.

7 Concerned with the enhancement of human well-being, social work attempts to relieve and prevent hardship and suffering. Social workers thus have a responsibility to help individuals, families, groups and communities through the provision and operation of appropriate services, and by contributing to social planning and action. Social work has developed methods of practice, which rely on a growing body of systematic knowledge and experience.

8 The social worker has a commitment to serve these purposes with integrity and skill. He acknowledges a professional obligation, not only to increase his personal knowledge and skill, but also to contribute to the total body of professional knowledge. This involves the constant evaluation of methods and policies in the light of changing needs. He recognises that the competence of his particular discipline is limited, and that the interests of the client require co-operation between those who share professional responsibility for the client's welfare.

9 The social worker's responsibility for relief and prevention of hardship and suffering is not always fully discharged by direct service to individual families and groups. He has the right and duty to bring to the attention of those in power, and of the general public, ways in which the activities of government, society or agencies create or contribute to hardship and suffering or militate against their relief. Social workers are often at the interface between powerful organisations and relatively powerless applicants for service. Certainly social workers are accountable to those under whose authority they work, and responsble for the efficient performance of their professional task and for their management of the organisation's resources. In view of the applicant's lack of power, social workers have a special responsibility to ensure the fullest possible realisation of his rights and satisfaction of his needs.

Principles of practice

10 In accepting the statement of principles embodying the primary obligations of the social worker, each Member of the Association undertakes that, to the best of his ability,

1 He will contribute to the formulation and implementation of policies for human welfare, and he will not permit his knowledge, skills or experience to be used to further inhuman policies.

2 He will respect his clients as individuals and will seek to ensure that their dignity, individuality, rights and responsibility shall be safeguarded.

3 He will not act selectively towards clients out of prejudice on the grounds of their origin, status, sex, sexual orientation, age, belief or contribution to society.

4 He will help his clients increase the range of choices open to them and their powers to make decisions.

5 He will not reject his client or lose concern for his suffering, even if obliged to protect others against him, or obliged to acknowledge an inability to help him.

6 He will give precedence to his professional responsibility over his personal interests.

7 He accepts that continuing professional education and training are basic to the practice of social work, and he holds himself responsible for the standards of service he gives.

8 He recognises the need to collaborate with others in the interests of his clients.

9 He will make clear in making any public statements or undertaking any public activities whether he is acting in a personal capacity or on behalf of an organisation.

10 He acknowledges a responsibility to help clients to obtain all those services and rights to which they are entitled, both from the agency in which he works and from any other appropriate source.

11 He recognises that information clearly entrusted for one purpose should not be used for another purpose without sanction. He respects the privacy of clients and confidential information about clients gained in his relationship with them or others. He will divulge such information only with

the consent of the client (or informant) except: where there is clear evidence of serious danger to the client, worker, other persons or the community, in other circumstances, judged exceptional, on the basis of professional consideration and consultation.

12 He will work for the creation and maintenance in employing agencies of conditions which enable social workers to accept the obligations of this Code.

Commentary on the Code of Ethics

1 The primary objectives of the Code are stated in para. 1: 'Objectives'. It attempts to be generally applicable, but not to stand for all time. New ideas about social work and changes in its environment will necessitate revision of the Code from time to time. The Code now presented is seen as an initial statement.

2 The Foreword (paras. 2–5) is a statement about the purposes of the Code. The Statement of Principles attempts to make explicit the values implicit in the practice of social work, and the Principles of Practice attempt to set out a basic Code for the individual social worker.

3 The Code of Ethics cannot be a manual of practice guidance. It must be couched in general terms, without being so general as to be incapable of application.

4 The Foreword expresses the view that the acceptance of special ethical obligations is part of the definition of any professional worker. This is the basic assumption which underlies any code of professional ethics (para. 2). Paragraph 3 challenges, as being oversimplifications, suggestions that the professional's only obligations are to the employer who hires him. Paragraph 4 refers to the rights of professionals. Chief among these is the right to exercise professional discretion.

On its statement of principles

On Paragraph 6:
Basic ethical principles in social work are necessarily extremely

wide in view of the wide focus of social work. A narrower basis than 'recognition of the value and dignity of every human being' would not be adequate. The social worker's basic values must relate to individuals, whether he works with individuals in a group or in communities, since it is the welfare of the individuals, in a group or community, which is the social worker's basic concern even if indirectly. The phrase 'irrespective of origin, status, sex, sexual orientation, age, belief or contribution to society' is intended to be interpreted widely. 'Origin' includes national, racial, social, cultural and class origins, distant or recent. 'Status' refers to an individual's current situation and includes social status, citizenship status and status in an institution or organisation. 'Age' does not mean old age only. 'Belief' is not confined to religious beliefs and includes beliefs which might be regarded as delusions.

The second sentence avoids the term 'self-determination', which sounds a little too open-ended and attempts to recognise the limitations which real-life situations impose. Social workers are often concerned with trying to harmonise conflicting interests and failing harmony, to arrive at the least damaging solution for all concerned. It is, therefore sometimes not possible to ensure that there will be no detriment to the interests of others, or to the client's interests. Hence the phrase 'with due regard for the interests of others'.

On Paragraph 7:
In the first sentence, limits to what social work can achieve have to be recognised. Being concerned with the enhancement of human well-being implies a responsibility to promote social functioning as well as to relieve suffering. The Codes of Ethics of the American and Canadian Associations state that the social worker renders appropriate services in a public emergency. All citizens are expected to do this and it is unnecessary to make this point specifically in relation to social workers. It is, however, covered in a general way by the reference to the relief of hardship and suffering.

On Paragraph 8:
In statements about obligations, commitments or responsibilities, it is important not to impose obligations which cannot be fulfilled. It is reasonable and proper to demand that social workers have integrity and skill. It would not be reasonable to demand, for example, that a social worker should feel sympathy for a particular

client, since feelings cannot be summoned at will. At the same time, it would be reasonable to expect the social worker to declare his position if the client aroused in him feelings which obstruct his capacity to help.

On Paragraph 9:
The first two sentences in this paragraph relate back to the statement in Paragraph 7 about social planning and action. The paragraph then comments on the social worker's own particular position in relation to planning, policy-making and the giving of service. The word 'interface' is intended to denote a place where contacts take place, contacts which may be active or passive and which may lead to harmony or to conflict. The paragraph goes on to try to balance the social worker's responsibility to his client. The client's frequent lack of power must be taken into account in weighing these responsibilities.

On its principles of practice

6 The principles of practice are based on and derived from the Statement of Principles, but are more personal and in more concrete terms. They move from general principles to guide practice, while recognising that social workers must exercise personal judgment. The preamble identifies the statement of principles as giving the primary, underlying or basic objectives of the social worker. All the undertakings which follow are qualified by the words 'to the best of his ability'. It is, therefore, recognised that, to take the first principle as an example, the opportunity to contribute to the formulation of policies may in a particular case be extremely limited. The social worker's willingness to give of his best is also recognised.

On principles 1–12

1 The Principle is fundamental. Observance of it may lead the social worker to resign his post in certain circumstances.
2 This Principle has general implications, but particular attention should be paid lest a person suffers loss of dignity or rights by the very act of becoming a client.

3 This Principle recognises that acting selectively is a morally neutral concept; in other words there are good reasons and bad reasons for acting selectively. It also recognises that no one is entirely free from prejudices. Objection can be taken only to selective or discriminatory action founded in prejudice. See also the comment on Paragraph 6.

4 This Principle holds good in all circumstances but it is sometimes necessary to help the client to abandon pseudo- or fantasy-choices so that effective choices may be made.

5 This Principle raises the problem of what can legitimately be said about the worker–client relationship. It is not possible to lay down requirements about the social worker's feelings, but 'rejection' includes action as well as feeling. Rejecting the client is, of course, different from closing the case. The reference to the need to protect others against the client does not cover all the situations in which the client may be in danger of rejection.

6 This Principle recognises the opportunities for conflict between personal interest and professional responsibilities. It places on the social worker an obligation not to pursue personal interests at the client's expense. It does not imply that at all times the social worker must put his responsibility to a client above his other responsibilities, for example, as a citizen or as a parent.

7 This Principle recognises that qualifying training does not complete a social worker's education. The importance of continuing education is also increased by the need to keep abreast of changing social factors. The assumption of personal responsibility for one's work is crucial to professionalism. A completely bureaucratised service cannot be a professional one.

8 This Principle places an obligation on social workers not only to be alert to the need to collaborate, but to take appropriate action.

11 This Principle has been distilled from the Association's Discussion Paper No. 1 on *Confidentiality in Social Work*, and for full consideration of the issues involved readers are referred to that Discussion Paper and subsequent statements.

The sanction referred to in the first sentence of the Principle is the sanction of the person giving the information to the social worker.

The multi-purpose agency, in particular, has to consider what administrative arrangements should be made to guard against the misuse of information.

The paper on confidentiality, after outlining situations in which the client's right to confidentiality might be overridden, states: 'In all the foregoing circumstances the breach of confidence must remain limited to the needs of the situation at that time and in no circumstances can the worker assume a carte blanche to reveal matters which are not relevant to that particular situation.'

12 There is a clear implication in this Principle that employers should recognise the whole Code. The Principle also acknowledges the difficulties of the employed professional, especially the social worker who works in an agency whose role is not specifically therapeutic.

Introduction

David Watson

I

Development of a Code of Ethics for any activity is a difficult intellectual task; having that Code accepted by a profesional association is a complex political achievement. The British Association of Social Workers completed this first step in 1975. But a Code of Ethics captures only a pause, and is always a potential focus for further debate.

Entry into debate about the appropriate content of a Code of Ethics is sometimes mistaken to reveal a certain sociological and political naivety. Over a number of years, sociologists have noticed that codes of ethics have a *function*: they embody an ideal of service which legitimises certain professional powers and privileges. This fact alone neither demonstrates nor warrants a cynical attitude *either* towards debate about the ideal embodied, *or* towards the professed commitment of the individuals concerned.

To take the latter first. As Wilding says, 'the essence of the professional claim . . . is that the main aim of the professions is not personal or collective profit and advantage, but service to their clients and to the community' (1982a, p. 77). Let us accept that it is also true that in our society 'the service ethic is a powerful justification of power and privilege' (Wilding, 1982a, p. 77), in the sense that a commitment to service is a necessary condition if power and privilege are to be thought justifiably conferred.

Certainly, in a society consistently committed to the equal distribution of political power, unequal power, privilege, a greater say than others have about what should be done (Singer, 1973, p. 36) might be granted to those with a socially useful expertise not widely distributed, only if they were willing to regulate use of that expertise in socially approved ways, that is, in accordance with an ideal of service.

In such a context is it likely also to be true that codes of ethics are 'political counters constructed as much to serve as public evidence of professional intentions and ideals as to provide actual behavioural guidelines for practitioners' (McKinlay, 1973, p. 308, reported in Wilding, 1982a, p. 77). But from all this *nothing* follows as regards the professed commitments of certain groups of workers.

More specifically, for example, it does not follow, as Wilding mistakenly presumes, that each profession is concerned 'to preserve the *reputation* for trustworthiness . . . because, without trust, the power – and privileges – of the professionals would become unacceptable and many cherished freedoms would have to be reined in' (1982a, pp. 76–7, emphasis added). Any concern with reputation may be quite indirect and concern be directly for that conscientious provision of service which justifies the trust and makes the corresponding reputation for trustworthiness well-founded. Codes of ethics which are 'political counters' may nevertheless embody an ideal of service followed to the letter, *or* they may embody an ideal largely ignored in practice. Identification of the function of codes of ethics is no measure of the degree of professional commitment to a code in practice: evidence, and explanation, of other kinds are needed (see Rees, 1978; Sainsbury *et al.*, 1982; Smith, 1980).

In either case, to return to my earlier, former point: evidence of conformity or non-conformity between actual professional behaviour and a code of ethics in no way vitiates discussion of the ideal of service appropriately embodied in the Code. On the contrary, critical appraisal of actual professional practice, and a serious concern for reform, presupposes a standard by which behaviour may be judged: that standard may be embodied in a code of ethics. So we come to take the second step.

2

The discussions collected in this book are not the views of the British Association of Social Workers, nor do all the contributors agree on all points. The second step is not the presentation of a united front, but initiation of a debate in which the obscurer parts of the Code will be explicitly interpreted, and the moral and political judgments implicit in it be exposed and explored.

Before I introduce the other contributions I should like to comment on two issues of continuing importance. First, the relation between judgment of need and expertise.

In a well-known and rarely criticised article (but see Clayton, 1983), Jonathan Bradshaw (1972) distinguishes the following ways of identifying need: *normative need*: a standard laid down by experts as desirable; *felt need*: equated with want, what people say they need, when asked; *expressed need*: demand, felt need turned into action; *comparative need*: not receiving a service received by others relevantly similar to you. Careless movement among these or other ways of identifying need has led some commentators to exasperation: 'the word "need" ought to be banished from discussion of public policy' (Culyer *et al.*, 1972). This would be a mistake, but clearly careless use is unhelpful. For that reason, the kind of discrimination of different uses which Bradshaw offers is to be welcomed (see Smith, 1980, ch. 3). What we should notice, however, which Bradshaw does not, is that three of his four ways of identifying need are utterly unreliable. 'Felt need' is an unreliable measure because, of course, a person may want, or, when asked, may say he needs, what he does not need; 'expressed need' is an unreliable measure because, of course, a person may demand what he does not need; and 'comparative need' is equally unreliable: from the fact that someone does not receive a service enjoyed by others like him, it does not follow that he is in need, since they may simply be recipients of a service they want but do not need. Felt need, expressed need and comparative need are reliable measures of need if and only if the people in question want, say they need, demand, or are in receipt of *only* what they need, which need we shall have to identify by some other means. Are standards laid down by experts, what Bradshaw calls 'normative need', any more reliable? Let us start out from a general conceptual point made by Brian Barry.

> Whenever someone says 'X is needed' it always makes sense . . . to ask what purpose it is needed for. Once an end is given it is . . . an 'objective' or 'scientific' matter to find out what conditions are necessary to bring it about . . . . (1965, pp. 47–8)

It is perhaps worth distancing oneself a little from Barry's confident assertion of what always makes sense. In a situation in which 'ordinary use' is inconsistent, a philosopher may helpfully clarify some particular use and recommend consistent adherence to it. Barry's concept of need is consistent with some but not all common uses and some strain will be felt. However, I adopt it because, as well as offering clarity, as any stipulative account might, it allows a simple account of the relation between expertise and the moral question of what ends are worthy of pursuit.

Thus: establishing need is a factual, not an evaluative matter: objective not subjective, but need is a fact which can be established only *after* the end, for which what is said to be needed as a means is given. In many cases such factual questions may be reliably answered, and so need be a matter best determined by those with knowledge of what is a means to given ends. Those with the requisite knowledge may or may not be few and far between; professionals dealing with such questions may not be a source of reliable answers, if their initial and continuing education is inadequate, and of course may not be the only possessors of the requisite expertise.

On the other hand, what ends are worthy of pursuit, and so what means should be considered for social support, is not a factual but a moral question. It follows that the name 'normative need' is misleadingly restricted to expert assessment. Felt, expressed, and comparative needs all presuppose valued purposes and are in that sense normative judgments of need. More importantly, it follows that what needs should be met by social provision, or by permitted private provision, is not a matter best determined by those with expertise on what is a means, because the answer to *this* question is a matter for judgment of a kind outside any expertise: moral judgment of what purposes are worthy of pursuit. What is a means, and the most efficient means to a given end, is best judged by those with the requisite knowledge, but that a given end is worthy of pursuit, or indeed that the most efficient, or the available, means to achieve it is morally acceptable, is not within the experts' proper authority.

Where authority to settle these social questions is located is a matter for one's political theory: the Sovereign, God, the People, or whoever, but in no case on the grounds of their special knowledge.

Let me sum up what I want to say about the relation between

judgment of need and expertise. Expertise, in the sense of special knowledge of what is a means, or the most efficient means, to a given end, is properly seen as at the service of whoever has authority to determine what purposes should receive social support. The experts will naturally have their own views, individually and collectively, on this latter question, and may seek authority to answer it on behalf of others, but that would be to seek a power to which their special knowledge gives no right.

The second issue on which I wish to comment is the relation between discretion and regulation. The existence of professional discretion is often said necessarily to subject clients to *arbitrary* decisions, and also necessarily to elevate a profession above public purposes. It seems to me that these assertions are mistaken, and I should like to show why using points made recently by Ronald Dworkin. We begin with the crucial general point that:

> the concept of discretion is at home in only one sort of context; when someone is in general charged with making decisions subject to standards set by a particular authority. It makes sense to speak of the discretion of a sergeant who is subject to orders of superiors, or the discretion of a sports official or contest judge who is governed by a rule book or the terms of the contest. Discretion, like the hole in a doughnut, does not exist except as an area left open by a surrounding belt of restriction. It is therefore a relative concept. It always makes sense to ask, 'Discretion under which standards?' . . . . (1978, p. 31)

If this is so, then far from there being an opposition between discretion and regulation, discretion can exist only in the context of regulation. However, as we shall see, those who suggest an opposition have in mind one kind of regulation in particular. But before we explore the alleged clash, let us note Dworkin's 'gross distinctions' among three senses of 'discretion'.

> Sometimes we use 'discretion' in a weak sense, simply to say that for some reason the standards an official must apply cannot be applied mechanically but demand the use of judgment. (1978, pp. 31–2)

For example, the command 'Take your five most experienced men' cannot be obeyed unless judgment is used to determine which are the five most experienced. In obeying the command, discretion in this weak sense must be exercised, but it is exercised within the context of restrictions set in the particular command to be obeyed.

> Sometimes we use the term in a different weak sense, to say only that some official has final authority to make a decision and cannot be reviewed and reversed by any other official . . . .' (1978, p. 32)

In this kind of case the final decision is a matter at the official's discretion, but discretion is again exercised within the context of restrictions, in this case determining these and not other matters to be at his discretion, on what occasions he may or must review the decisions of his inferiors, and so on.

> I call both of these senses weak to distinguish them from a stronger sense . . . to say that on some issue (someone) is simply not bound by standards set by the authority in question. (1978, p. 32)

The command 'Pick any five men for patrol' grants discretion in the stronger sense in that no standards have been set, as they were by addition of the word 'experienced', by which the men must be chosen: the standards set don't extend so far or purport to control such issues as whether or not experienced men are to be preferred. There is one final point to note:

> The strong sense of discretion is not tantamount to license, and does not exclude criticism. Almost any situation in which a person acts . . . makes relevant certain standards of rationality, fairness, and effectiveness. (1978, p. 33)

In the previous example, the sergeant may choose any five for patrol, but he may choose stupidly, maliciously or carelessly and, if he does so, though he was not disobedient he nevertheless behaved in a way which may be criticised.

To return to the alleged clash between discretion and regulation, a recent basic textbook for students of social administration introduced the clash as follows:

> While there is probably fairly general agreement that the system of individual welfare rights that has been built up over the years should not be dismantled, there is still dispute at the margin about whether the right balance has been achieved between

legalism and discretion . . . by legalism is meant the allocation of welfare benefits or services on the basis of legal rules and precedent. By discretion is meant the allocation of welfare benefits or services on the basis of individual judgments. (Jones *et al.*, 1978, p. 140)

On Dworkin's analysis there can be no balance *thus described* to achieve: legalism, as described, itself *requires* 'individual judgments' to be made. Welfare benefits or services allocated on the basis of legal rules and precedent cannot literally be allocated mechanically. Even in those cases which 'obviously' fall under a particular rule, to establish that they are uncontroversial and can be quickly dealt with itself requires judgment: discretion in the first weak sense identified by Dworkin has been exercised. Further, legalism requires the existence of second-order rules allocating authority to allocate welfare benefits or services (see Downie, 1971, p. 78), and so entails granting some official final authority to make a decision: discretion in the second weak sense must be exercised. Far from being incompatible with the existence of discretion in the distribution of welfare benefits or services, legal regulation *introduces* two contexts in which discretion must be exercised. If we must talk of a balance between legalism and discretion, it must be a question of the appropriate extent of legal regulation, with no suggestion that legal regulation ends discretion.

Legal regulation is quite compatible with discretion in the stronger sense: legal rules may avoid setting standards on particular questions. However, in so far as legal rules allow discretion in the stronger sense they obviously weakly restrict those authorised to implement them. A number of comments might be made in defence of some legal regulation of this less restricting kind. First a reminder that the discretion to be exercised is within 'a surrounding belt of restriction' set by standards of rationality, fairness and effectiveness. Professionals are not beyond severe criticism even where they follow to the letter legal rules allowing them discretion in the strong sense. Their decisions in such cases are not arbitrary, but manifest their own standards of rationality, fairness, or effectiveness, and their standards may be challenged.

Nor is the 'consumer of welfare' changed from 'a citizen claiming his legal entitlement' into 'a supplicant beholden to the giver' (Jones *et al.*, 1978, p. 141). A client's capacity and opportunity for effective criticism of the standards of rationality, fairness or effectiveness of a decision is not removed by the existence of discretion in the strong sense, though in a society in which the conceptual resources for social relationships in general, and for conflict and conciliation in particular, are relatively limited, that capacity and opportunity will be dramatically eroded: in a society in which the most effective form of dispute resolution involves recourse to law, and in which 'supplicant' is the only status alternative to 'citizen', this will certainly be true.

Further, the existence of discretion in the strong sense does not preclude subordination of the decision-making of a profession to public purposes. Again, the capacity and opportunity for effective criticism of the standards of rationality, fairness or effectiveness of decisions is not removed, from those who wish to argue that the decisions made threaten public purposes, by the mere existence of discretion in the strong sense. The development, and impact, of the critical capacities and opportunities of clients and guardians of public purposes are a function of *other* features of the context in which decisions are made. Discretion in the strong sense is compatible with a practice fully recognising accountability to individuals subject to the decisions made and to society. Of course, professionals and others with such discretion cannot be compelled in their decision-making and may continue in irrational, unfair or ineffective practice, so perhaps we should conclude that discretion in the strong sense should rarely be granted in a society, like ours, in which accountability beyond legal requirement is so impoverished.

3

The contributors to this book raise and discuss many points worthy of further consideration. Let me simply pick out some amongst those raised by each author. In chapter 1 I shall argue that social work practice is invariably normative and that therefore a Code of Ethics is useful if it makes explicit the ends and means to which practitioners are committed. Not that the ends or means are beyond dispute, and I also argue that the nature of social work, and therefore its aims, cannot be discovered simply by observation of what is done by those employed as 'social workers', nor by noting what is said by a professional association. Our conception of what social work is must be sufficiently independent to allow critical discussion of such practice and such pronouncements.

Participation in development of such an independent conception, and its implementation, requires a certain kind of preparation for social work. In her chapter, Ruth Wilkes distinguishes between education and training. Education, unlike job-oriented training, encourages reflection rather than replication, and tolerates disagreement, fitting the social worker to take personal responsibility for wqrk in the context of discretion in the strong sense described earlier, and responsibility for maintenance of justifiable standards of rationality, fairness and effectiveness.

In chapter 3, Neil Leighton draws attention to the distinction between personal and professional commitments. The distinction sustains the possibility of divided loyalties in social work practice. Professional social workers have no mandate to implement personal values which are not professional values in their work; if they do, and in so far as those personal values are shared with others, they may practice a recognisable type of social work – Christian, marxist, feminist, or whatever – but are unlikely for that reason to manifest values shared by members of the profession as such. Further, in so far as the distinction is blurred, in use of the relationship between himself and the client, the social worker is in danger of deceiving the client about its nature. As Strawson would put it: it may be taken for a reactive rather than an objective relationship (see Strawson, 1968), and inappropriate criteria of rationality, fairness, and effectiveness applied in assessing that relationship.

In chapter 4, Gavin Fairbairn distinguishes a number of senses in which a social worker might be 'responsible', and is particularly concerned to criticise a misunderstanding of the kind of responsibility which is being liable to give an account of one's actions. If accountability is reduced simply to being the bearer of blame when things go wrong, whether one is responsible in other senses or not, then considerable harms to clients are likely. Discretion will not be used to create opportunities for the development of client autonomy, but to close off accusations of incaution.

Such a perversion of accountability is more likely when social workers lack an independent conception of their task and independence of mind. But few of their aims can be realised without good working relationships with colleagues in social work, their managers, and workers in other fields. Independence must co-exist with collaboration. If we do take the view that social work should be subordinated to public purposes, we must consider how public purposes are to be recognised. If public purposes are discovered by opinion poll or general elections, then public purposes may not be in the public interest, since a people, like an individual, may mistake its interests (Barry, 1964). How can collaboration be sustained when we judge departmental, local or national government policies seriously harmful to our clients? Loyalties may thus be divided between clients and employer or government. They may also be divided between one's clients in general and a particular client, where some policy favours most clients but not this one in particular. As Malcolm Payne argues in chapter 5, the Code must be developed to deal more helpfully with issues of this kind.

Huw Richards, in chapter 6, argues for a broader conception of social work, so as to include non-professional efforts by a wide range of 'carers', including clients themselves. In particular he argues for greater emphasis on support for clients in their own pursuit of rights. Various 'declarations' of rights might be appended to the Code and invoked in challenging policy. This strategy extends client access to standards of fairness, strengthening their armoury in holding policy-makers accountable. Those who prefer their clients or social workers obediently following past practice and present instructions will not relish such a picture, but on what *grounds* can it be resisted by a society committed to self-realisation?

In the chapter which follows, John Hudson considers a range of issues raised for the Code in the context of residential social work. What I want to pick out here is the discussion of the concepts of 'social worker' and 'client' in such a setting. In permeable residential homes family members and others are drawn into participation in care, and a broader conception of social work and of the application of the Code come to seem most appropriate. Work with families can also make the identified client less clearly the client.

We conclude with a short comment by Joan Sutherland arguing, amongst other things, for the Code to be more firmly conceived as regulating professional activity, with sanctions attached, and asserting the legitimacy of the interest of colleagues and clients in an explicit statement of ends to be pursued and means employed.

Many more issues are discussed than those to which I have drawn attention. The second step requires a willingness to raise and reflect upon the moral point of view from which social work ought to be practised, so that standards of rationality, fairness and effectiveness may be asserted with integrity, and public accountability welcomed.

What's the point of A Code of Ethics for Social Work?

David Watson

Introduction

According to A Code of Ethics for Social Work (BASW, 1975, para. 1), the primary objective of the code of ethics there presented is to make the ethical principles implicit in professional practice explicit for the protection of clients. On what grounds might this claim plausibly be made? In Part One of my discussion I shall describe the kind of conception of professional social work upon which such a statement logically depends, say something about the logical limits to *sources* for any conception of professional social work, and identify the types of supporting beliefs which give the BASW Code of Ethics its rationale. I shall then discuss the criticism that the level of abstraction employed in the Code of Ethics is too high, consider proposals to meet such criticism, and consider the implications of those proposals for professional discretion. Finally, I shall say something about the relationship between a code of ethics and disciplinary procedures.

What makes the code make sense?

1

What we may take to be the point of any code of ethics for social work practice entirely depends upon our conception of the nature of social work: that is the linchpin of the framework of thoughts supporting any statement of the objectives of such a code. So this is where I want to begin. As we proceed we must consider points made in a debate which is already well underway, and which features competing conceptions of social work. By some, social work is conceived so broadly as to include every form of 'caring for strangers' (Barclay, 1982, para. 15), 'everything done to help a fellow being in trouble by anyone who does not owe a duty as a relative or close friend' (Barclay, para. 14). However, the BASW Code is concerned with 'the professional practice of social work', with social work more narrowly conceived as 'a professional activity' (1975a, para. 1). In chapter 6 of this book, Huw Richards argues that the Code should be developed so that it is a useful guide to the responsibilities, and rights, of the non-professionals who engage in social work more broadly conceived. However, here I consider the Code with the narrower focus it currently declares.

In developing the narrower conception of social work, with reason authors draw upon what we know of the role and tasks of those in the paid occupation called 'social work', those employed by local authorities or voluntary agencies, perhaps to provide help to people with certain kinds of practical or emotional or behavioural problems (Barclay, para. 18; but see also Sainsbury *et al.*, 1982). But we must not rely too heavily upon what we know those in that paid occupation to do; they may face demands and constraints which make it unlikely that a role can be maintained with the coherence and consistency necessary if a conception of *professional* social work is to be observed in practice. The conception developed must have a life of its own, independent of what those in the paid occupation do, if what they do is to be described discriminatingly. It must be logically *possible* for us to conclude, after empirical investigation, that what those in the paid occupation called 'social work' do is not professional social work *at all* on our conception of it, or, more likely, that what they do is professional social work only in part: what they do includes some but not only professional social work tasks. For example, in the Barclay Report the activities of 'counselling' and 'social care planning' are presented as 'the formal aspect of social work'. That is, in the view of the Working Party these activities are what professional social work is, and how those in the paid occupation must spend their time to *warrant* their description as 'professional social workers'. Of course, those in the paid occupation called 'social work' may be required to perform other tasks: in day and residential services such people often perform tasks which may be grouped under the headings 'tending', 'providing satisfying experiences for clients', and 'maintaining clients' links with the community', which are not in themselves what the Working Party recognise as 'formal social work tasks'; so those there employed as social workers are engaged in professional social work only in part, and *diverted* from such work by these other activities, *except* where these are the best means of fulfilling their proper tasks (paras. 4.42–4.47), or a necessary means (like sharpening a pencil to draw up an agenda for social care planning).

All of this has interesting implications for social work education which can only be hinted at here. If you take what is done by those in the paid occupation to be definitive of the nature of social work, then your conception of social work, and preparation for it, must be profoundly conservative. Education is reduced to training in what is done. Only an independent conception opens up the possibility of critical judgment of what is done, though this will be caricatured as reflecting 'a professional idealisation of the work to be done . . . rather than the work as it actually is' (Wilding, 1982a, p. 55).

The first point to note, then, is that our conception of social work cannot simply be derived from the observed practice of 'social workers', for we cannot investigate and determine when it is true that those in the paid occupation are engaged in professional social work unless we possess a conception of it independent of the activities of those in the paid occupation by which to discriminate observation of activities which do constitute professional social work from observation of activities which do not.[1]

The second point to note is that conceptions of social work, including those of professional social work, are invariably *normative*. The BASW Code begins by asserting that ethical principles are implicit in the practice of professional social work. I want to endorse this, but add that this is true for social work, professional or otherwise, and unavoidable. A normative conception of an activity is one which ties its identity to the pursuit of certain valued purposes: good social work is the rational pursuit,[2] and bad social work the irrational pursuit of those purposes; in the absence of pursuit of those purposes, you are not practising social work at all. One may take the view that 'the function of social workers is to enable, empower, support and encourage, but not usually to take over from social networks' (Barclay, para 13.43), or, emphasising ends rather than means, that 'social work attempts to relieve and prevent hardship and suffering' (Statement of Principles, para. 7). These are, of course, incomplete statements of a conception, hardly distinguishing professional social work from most forms of caring: something must be said about the particular types of network, hardship or suffering in question, and the knowledge and skills appropriate to their encouragement and relief, respectively. However, in all cases social work is thought of as something those in the paid occupation *ought* to practice, as a means to worthwhile ends.

To our present discussion, the importance of noting the normative nature of conceptions of social work, and in due course the kind of evaluations they turn out to include, is obvious: it makes sense of the claim that ethical principles are implicit in the professional practice of social work, as they are in any notion of a practice of social work. Further, in this context *a code of ethics* for professional social work practice has point: given a normative and positive conception of professional social work, proposals for the regulation of the paid occupation, so that practice might satisfy the conception, are only to be expected. A code of ethics identifies those principles and purposes which shall govern its adherents in their work, and it declares a point of view from which their practice might be judged. As the BASW Code says (Objectives, para. 1), the Code makes explicit the ethical principles implicit in professional practice. We have yet to see why it might also be claimed that those principles should be made explicit 'for the protection of clients'.

However, let me first develop the general implications of the normative nature of conceptions of social work for the *content* of any code. Given that what is to count as social work practice depends upon what objectives are thought worthwhile, people committed to social work practice are committed to ethical principles which declare that certain purposes ought to be realised. If they are to play their part, they must be committed to the discovery of the means of achieving those purposes, and to their own acquisition of the necesary knowledge and skills. Their commitment inevitably places upon them a responsibility to act with certain ends in view, and to ensure that the component activities of their practice are means to those ends. As the Code says in relation to professional social work, the implicit ethical principles 'prescribe the professional responsibility of the social worker' (Objectives, para. 1). The Code's Statement of Principles has just the predicted content. The end in view for which 'the professional accepts a responsibility' is stated in paragraph 6: the self-realisation of the individual person with due regard for the interest of others. The commitment to discovery of the means and acquisition of the necessary skills is alleged, in paragraph 7, to have been fulfilled to an extent which allows social workers to carry 'responsibility to help . . . through the provision of appropriate services', which they are in a position to identify. The further paragraphs of the Statement of Principles, and the Principles of Practice, elaborate the implications of commitment to the central purpose of social work, as here conceived, and of commitment to playing one's part, whatever one thinks of the elaborations (see Nielson, 1976).

In so far as the necessary knowledge and skills are narrowly distributed, the responsibility to achieve the purposes in question 'through the provision and operation of appropriate services' does not fall upon everyone. Those with any necesary expertise, and committed to social work practice, acquire special obligations, as the Foreword and the Commentary on it assert. They carry the responsibility to pursue the broad purpose of the activity by the means at only their disposal. Expertise and commitment to its exercise yield 'obligations beyond those of the ordinary citizen' (Foreword, para. 2), and, as expected, are accompanied in the Code by assertion of special rights alleged necessary to fulfilment of those obligations (Foreword, paras. 4 and 5; Commentary, para. 4).

However, it may be worth stressing that though 'acceptance of special ethical obligations is part of the definition of any profess-ional worker' (sic. Commentary, para. 4), it is only part. The other part is the obligation to pursue a broad purpose which might be pursued by non-professionals, and by other professionals by very different means. Further, the special obligations are themselves derived in part from that un-special obligation: they are obligations to pursue the broad purpose in contexts to which only they have access. Social workers do not espouse principles and purposes unique to professional social work. The principles may be *basic* to the profession of social work (Statement of Principles, para. 6) but hardly *exclusive* to it or any profession. Rather, they commit themselves to putting those principles into practice in a restricted range of settings. This is the kindest way to take the statement that 'acceptance of special ethical obligations is part of the definition of any professional worker' (Commentary, para. 4). It would be less kind, though quite natural, to take this BASW statement to claim that the principles and purpose made explicit in the Code *are* distinctive of professional social work, or their acceptance distinctive of the professional social worker. The principles must be made much more specific if such a claim is to be sustained. How could professional social workers seriously arrogate to themselves 'the recognition of the value and dignity of every human being . . .' (Statement of Principles, para. 6)? What is basic to professional social work might of course guide activities of many other kinds. And it is as well that this is so. In committing themselves to such a code of ethics, those in the paid occupation identify themselves as standing where others also stand, and might then with more prospect seek authority to practice, having declared their commitment to use of their skills and knowledge to what others may also regard as good purpose.

2

Before coming to the relation between the Code and the protection of clients, I'd like to make a number of related points about phrases used in the BASW Code, and elsewhere, which are sources of confusion. I have spoken of a social worker's commitment to a code of ethics as his acknowledging an obligation to practise in ways satisfying a particular conception of professional social work. The BASW Code describes such a social worker as acknowledging a 'professional obligation' (Statement of Principles, para. 8), and the Code itself as prescribing 'the professional responsibility of the social worker' (Objectives, para. 1). These phrases are dangerous. I should like to identify the danger through some comments on the idea of 'membership of a profession'.

It seems to me that commitment to some code of ethics is a necessary though not a sufficient condition of membership of a profession,[3] so that *if* other conditions are also satisfied, we may describe social workers, committed to practice within a code making explicit the principles and purposes implicit in a particular conception of professional social work, as 'members of the social work profession'.[4] The social workers in question take on an obligation to put the conception into practice, and as I've already suggested, if practised in settings closed to the ordinary citizen, professional social work practice would illustrate the fact that in such a society, at least, 'membership of any profession entails certain obligations beyond those of the ordinary citizen' (Foreword, para. 2), though there may be some obligations falling upon both the professional and the ordinary citizen. Both may be under an obligation to cause no unnecessary suffering, but only the professional social worker may be under obligation to prepare a social enquiry report, say.

We may distinguish between 'membership of a profession' and 'membership of a professional association': membership of a professional association is neither a necessary nor a sufficient condition of membership of a profession; the creation of an association *presupposes* the existence of members of a profession, members in virtue, amongst other things, of their commitment to a code of ethics implicit in a conception, in this case, of professional social work. The two memberships are easily confused where a professional association exists to promote the interests (not necesarily self-interest)[5] of members of a profession, where those members articulate the code implicit in their conception of professional social work, and where members of the professional association are required to uphold that code. However, our conception of professional social work, and the obligations implicit in it, must be as independent of the pronouncements of any professional association as of the practice of those in the paid occupation, and for the same reason. The pronouncements of a professional association cannot be taken as definitive of the best conception of professional practice, nor of the obligations implied by any conception.

The distinction between these two memberships makes the expressions 'professional responsibility' and 'professional obligation' ambiguous. Our professional responsibilities may be those we bear as members of a profession or those we bear as members of a professional association. The former are those implicit in our conception of professional social work and will be included in the latter, so long as the professional association makes them explicit in its Code of Ethics, otherwise not. In general, in the BASW Code these phrases may be taken to refer to responsibilities borne as members of a profession, though paragraph 5 highlights the problem in saying 'Any professional association has the duty to secure, as far as possible, that its members discharge their professional obligations', since it will surely be the duty of any professional association to secure that its members discharge the responsibilities they bear as members of that association as well as those they bear as members of a profession, and those responsibilities may conflict. If we forget that responsibilities as a member of a profession have a life of their own, independent of the pronouncements of a professional association, we shall also forget that at times we may have *divided* loyalties and cannot fulfil our obligations to our professional association, and fellow members of it, and at the same time fulfil our obligation to practise professional social work. A call to strike offers a sharp reminder of this possibility. In such cases it may be argued that loyalties are not divided: the obligation to practice professional social work is best fulfilled, in the longer run, by fulfilling obligations incurred as a member of a professional association. This is often the case, but it is not a necessity.

It is worth observing here that the criticism that 'codes of behaviour can be said to diminish individual responsibility . . . by prescribing what is permitted and forbidden' (CCETSW, 1976, para. 5.07), is based on a misunderstanding of the possibility of conflict between one's obligations as a member of a profession and as a member of a professional association. Even if such conflicts were *always* resolved by giving priority to our obligations as members of a professional association, if we make that a *rule*, we retain individual responsibility for our membership of that association, and usually some individual responsibility for its policies. Paradoxically for such critics, the BASW Code stresses *continued* individual responsibility: 'the assumption of personal responsibility for one's work is crucial to professionalism' (Commentary, On Principles, para. 7); the professional social worker is committed to 'constant evaluation of methods and policies in the light of changing needs' (Statement of Principles, para. 8) (including the method of constant evaluation?) presumably including those of his professional association. In the BASW Code at least, 'the right to exercise professional discretion' clearly leaves the individual social worker with responsibility to determine priority when his obligations as a member of a profession conflict with his obligations as a member of a professional association.

3

Let us return to our earlier discussion. I said that conceptions of professional social work are invariably normative, and that, given a conception that is also positive, proposals for the regulation of practice by reference to a code of ethics are only to be expected. I now add that conceptions of professional social work are invariably positive. Criticism focuses on social work practice: in some particular case, or perhaps in general, those in the paid occupation are said not to practise what they preach (Smith, 1980, amongst others). To conceive of professional social work negatively would indeed be to make a code of ethics for professional practice out of place. What ought not to be done is something that simply ought not to be done, not something that ought to be done ethically. Something might be called 'a good murder' because it was a skilful killing, but hardly because it was done with due attention to a code of ethics for such activities. Some may baulk at the idea of a normative conception of social work: those who tell their growing children 'We don't discuss religion or politics in this house, it only causes trouble'. Relief from implicit commitments may seem to be available thanks to the level of abstraction so far employed: commitment to the relief of suffering (Statement of Principles, para. 7) may or may not be commitment to social change. I shall return to discussion of the level of abstraction in Part Two. One might also stress the skills and knowledge necessary to, and perhaps distinctive of, professional social work, suggesting that professional social work is to be recognised by methods rather than purposes, among which it may be neutral. However, there's no refuge here from a normative conception: the skills and knowledge necessary are *identified* by reference to what we believe to be the activities those in the paid occupation ought to put into practice, so that certain purposes may be realised.

Elaborations of conceptions of professional social work do usually include some kind of account of the skills and knowledge necessary if social work thus conceived is to be practised. The BASW Code says of the professional social worker that 'he accepts that continuing professional education and training are basic to the practice of social work' (Principles of Practice, para. 10.7). The skills and knowledge in question being those necessary if he is to play his part in fulfilling the objectives outlined in the Statement of Principles, paragraphs 6 and 7, including the responsibility 'to help individuals, families, groups and communities through the provision and operation of appropriate services'. In slightly more detail it may be suggested that for professional social work to be practised 'three sorts of skill are needed – skills in human relationships; skills in analysis (assessing people, analysing situtations and evaluating the effects of action taken); and skills in effectiveness (carrying out action planned)' (Barclay, para. 10.23). Further, 'skills such as we see to be demanded by social workers presuppose possession of knowledge of two kinds: practical information for immediate use, and knowledge that provides insight into the behaviour of people, organisations and societies, and into how behaviour is likely to change under the influence of alternative courses of action' (Barclay, para. 10.27). As outlined, of course, these accounts are insufficiently specified to pick out the skills and knowledge necessary in practice of professional social work.

The implied skills and knowledge may be more or less accessible, and so more or less suited to unsupervised use. If what professional social workers have to offer is little understood by non-social workers (Barclay, para. 12.8) and such undrestanding not quickly achieved, then those from whom the professional social worker derives his authority to act, a court, client or whoever, will be ill-placed in a number of important respects: to judge the need for professional social work services; to compare with alternatives what professional social work or any particular agency or worker has to offer; to judge the quality of the service actually delivered. In this context, again, a code of ethics for social work practice has point: given a conception of professional social work implying use of relatively inaccessible skills and knowledge, authority to act is to some extent granted on trust; a code of ethics, as I said earlier, identifies those principles and purposes which shall govern its adherents in their work, and it declares a point of view from which their practice may be judged, so that trust is reserved for those in whom trust can be justified: those committed to using the skills and knowledge in question to good purpose.

This provides some ground for the claim that the principles and purposes implicit in professional practice should be made explicit 'for the protection of clients', at least as far as voluntary clients are concerned. If it is made explicit what principles are to be followed, and purposes pursued, in the professional social worker–client relationship, then the voluntary client can protect himself from social workers with aims he does not share. Those clients receiving attention from the agency against their wishes are less obviously protected by a code. What they may want most is protection from social workers. Even so, a code may play a part in protecting both types of client from social workers acting unprofessionally, to which they, or those authorising any 'compulsory care', might object.

Again, we must remember that clients are 'relatively powerless applicants for service' (Statement of Principles, para. 9); professional social workers seek authority to give or withhold scarce resources, including their own time (Commentary, para. 4, and Commentary, On Principles, para. 7); the counselling and social care planning in which professional social workers engage, demands from the client disclosures which increase his vulnerability, and so on. If our conception of professional social work makes reference to clients so at risk, to social workers engaged in 'social policing' (Barclay, para. 10.11) and 'gatekeeping' (para. 3.52), then a code of ethics which identifies those principles and purposes which shall govern its adherents in their work, and declares a point of view from which their practice may be judged, may be said to go *some* way towards the protection of clients.

4

Summary of Part One

I have drawn attention to the normative and positive nature of conceptions of professional social work which provide grounds for a code of ethics, regulating the paid occupation so that such good work may be identified and practised, and bad work castigated. I have also argued that our conception of professional social work must be independent of what those in the paid occupation do, and what those in the professional association say, even if we draw upon these sources. Finally, I have identified those beliefs, about the skills and knowledge necessary to professional social work, and about its clientele, which allow us to describe a code making explicit the principles and purposes of professional social work as 'for the protection of clients'.

Part Two: The protection of clients

1

'For the protection of yourselves, more like' say the cynics, given that popular belief in professional integrity keeps the clients coming through the door, and so the bread buttered, and given that whenever a dissatisfied client alleges misconduct or incompetence, the 'protectors' seem to close ranks.

Let us now turn to criticisms of the BASW Code which start out by drawing attention to its level of abstraction. These criticisms raise issues of importance because they are likely to apply to any code of ethics. There's no denying the level of abstraction in some parts of the account of the principles and purposes of professional social work: it involves 'recognition of the value and dignity of every human being' (Statement of Principles, para. 6), and is 'concerned with the enhancement of human well-being . . . through the provision and operation of appropriate services' (Statement of Principles, para. 7). But this level of abstraction is not uniformly employed. The principle of confidentiality is outlined in more detail (Principles of Practice, para. 10.11), and that discussion is itself derived from a more detailed Discussion Paper to which we are referred (Commentary, On Principles, para. 11). Again, the statement of what does *not* detract from the value and dignity of a human being is surely sufficiently specific: origin, status, sex, sexual orientation, age, belief or contribution to society (Statement of Principles, para. 6), particularly when supplemented in the Commentary: ' "Origin" includes national, racial, social, cultural and class origins . . .' and so on. Further, surely we take the point that 'basic ethical principles are necessarily extremely wide, in view of the wide focus of social work' (Commentary, On its Statement of Principles, on Paragraph 6), and agree that 'the Code of Ethics cannot be a manual of practice guidance. It must be couched in general terms, without being so general as to be incapable of application' (Commentary, para. 3).

What some critics fear, however, is not principles and purposes described in such abstract terms as to be *incapable* of application, but principles and purposes described in such abstract terms as to be capable of application in *a number* of ways, only *some* of which are consistent with the conception of professional social work to which those in the paid occupation may commit themselves. In that case talk of the Code guiding the practice of those in the paid occupation seems generous, and the value of the Code in protecting clients is diminished. If descriptions of the principles and purposes implicit in our conception of professional social work are so abstract, then that conception is implied to be correspondingly undiscriminating. It might not discriminate tending (Parker, 1981) from counselling, for example, since both may express 'recognition of the value and dignity of a human being', 'facilitate self-realisation' and 'relieve suffering'. In so far as we possess a more discriminating conception of professional social work, highly abstract principles and purposes do a disservice to clients in need of professional social work more narrowly conceived, by legitimating the diversion of resources from such work.

Again, it is certainly true, though rather non-directive, to say that the professional social worker must 'keep abreast of changing social factors' (Commentary, On Principles, para. 7), and that it will therefore continue to be necessary for him to 'exercise personal judgment' (Commentary, On its Principles of Practice, para. 6): the professional social worker not only has a right to exercise professional discretion, it seems, but also a personal duty to exercise that discretion on the frequent occasions when the Code can guide him no further. Even so, a code should surely be specific enough to exclude some practice which may be 'caring for strangers', but is hardly professional social work. What can be done?

A rather abstract Code may be associated with supplementary material which makes clear to those familiar with it specifically which, of the various practices that might come under too abstract Code descriptions, may be in question. The implied conception of professional social work is then indicated by a reading of the Code supplemented by such material. I am thinking of material like the many CCETSW Reports on aspects of the professional social work task, the Barclay Report, and more closely related to the BASW Code, BASW's own discussion papers: Discussion Paper No. 1 on *Confidentiality* is referred to in the Code as such supplementary material. This is to admit the inadequacy of the Code itself, and so it might be suggested that a better remedy than supplementation would be a Code which was not abstract but specific. However, given the range of settings to be governed, and the continued changes within those settings, a specific code would at any time be *very* long and soon out of date. It seems to me that supplementation better recognises that while agreement might be reached on relatively abstract principles, a Code must always be *developing*, and its application a subject for *debate*: the supplementary material can direct and contribute to that debate.

Supervised training is another available strategy: the trainee being supposed to 'catch on' to the more precise conception of professional social work by observing it put into practice, and having his own practice corrected by those who have grasped the conception.

However, such strategies demand more patience than some can muster. The discussion papers may not be read, and supervision may be insufficiently directive. If professional social work practice by those in the paid occupation is to be *secured*, it may be said, what is expected must be spelled out in legislation governing social work, and in contracts of employment. In the context of such regulation, a Code of Ethics would be superfluous. Those who take this view note with regret that 'all health and welfare professions which entail a practitioner/client relationship subject to a code of professional conduct and who carry responsibility for meeting the needs of individuals and serving the interests of communities (and not only for administrative purposes) are subject to statutory regulation of training *and* of practice, except social workers' (Malherbe, quoted in Barclay, para. 12.9; see also para. 2.4).

Such an approach would certainly give any probationary period (Barclay, para. 12.37), or 'independent inspectorate which would monitor the practice of both social workers and their employing agencies' (Barclay, para. 12.39), some bite. Even so, it would not follow that 'the first duty of a social worker is to do his job within the terms of reference presented by his local authority' (Pinker, in Barclay, p. 244). It *may* be true that 'he is solely accountable to his local authority in a legal and contractual sense' (Pinker, in Barclay, p. 244), if the law and his contract of employment make it so, but he may continue to have duties which take priority, namely, those obligations he incurs as a member of the social work profession. I said earlier that the conception of professional social work we adopt must be independent of what those in the paid occupation do, if we are to discriminate between occasions when they *are* and when they *are not* engaged in professional social work. This remains true even when *we* are in the paid occupation, and the law and our contract of employment *tell* us what to do. Such independence of conception sustains the possibility of critical review of changing laws, contracts of employment, and instructions. Put it another way: a contract of employment specifying the professional social work task in detail protects the client's right to what *the contract* says is professional social work. Further, even though the terms of our employment have been freely contracted, it is too easy just to say to the professional social worker, torn between his contractual obligations and those implicit in his conception of professional social work, that he ought to resign (Pinker, in Barclay, p. 244). Where professional social work can be practised on any scale only in contract with an employer with a near monopoly of supply, it will often be the case that his obligations as a member of a profession are best fulfilled if he stays to fight for, and wins, a change in his contractual obligations, through participation in collective action in collaboration with fellow employees.

2

Extensive specification of the professional social work task can only take us so far. The principles are applied, and purposes pursued, in a changing social environment. There will always be the require-ment to exercise judgment; to ask, does professional social work in these circumstances imply doing this, or that? It will always be open for someone to argue that circumstances are sufficiently changed to make your judgments mistaken though not always convincingly. This brings me to further comment I should like to make on the idea of professional discretion, and which will lead into other comments on the protection of clients from unprofessional conduct.

I have said that there is a continuing requirement that judgment be exercised. I take professional discretion to be exercised in this context when professional social workers make judgments concern-ing the appropriateness of certain forms of intervention. However, given the possibility of disagreement in judgment among pro-fessionals, and a tendency to describe such judgments in any case as 'personal' (Commentary, On it Principles of Practice, para. 6), 'subjective', or 'arbitrary' (Barclay, paras. 7.21, 12.62), the spectre of unjustifiable, anarchic decision-making haunts us, and may tempt us to mistake where our first duty lies. Such fears are misplaced.

To begin with, conceptions of professional social work, or anything else, are not personal, private or subjective in any of the senses from which the spectre draws life, but *public*. Establishing a standard for use of the expression 'professional social work', what is to count as professional social work, 'is not an activity which it makes sense to ascribe to any individual in complete isolation from other individuals. For it is contact with other individuals which alone makes possible the external check on one's actions which is inseparable from an established standard' (Winch, 1958, p. 32; Watson, 1981). Conceptions of professional social work have a life only within a linguistic community, and members of the profession will be prominent, but not the only, members of that community. Professional discretion is not the exercise of arbitrary judgment, but the application of an established conception in new circumstances, and one's judgment subject to external check by other individuals to whom one is accountable as fellow members of that linguistic community, if as nothing else. As I pointed out in my Introduction to this book, quoting Dworkin, 'Discretion like the hole in a doughnut, does not exist except as an area left open by a surrounding belt of restriction' (Dworkin, 1978, p. 31), and however free, or unfree, professional social workers are from legal and contractual restriction, whatever professional discretion remains is *not* tantamount to licence, and does *not* exclude criticism in terms of certain standards of rationality, fairness and effectiveness (Dworkin, p. 33) by members of the profession *and* the wider society in which they act, and by reference to the broad purposes to which professional practice is said to be directed, though professions may achieve social positions which remove any requirement to *heed* that criticism.

This point about professional accountability for exercise of discretion is worth enlarging in the context of questions about the relationship between the Code of Ethics and disciplinary procedures. Can clients be protected from violations of the Code? It is clear that professional social work practice cannot be guaranteed. It is also clear that in the absence of full-time non-disruptive surveillance, this type of work is best and most extensively promoted by those things that sustain the growth and development of *self*-regulated commitment to a conception of professional social work, by those in the paid occupation; items ranging from case-conference in which conceptions, and their implications for practice in a particular case, are explored with others, even to academic discussions like this. Such things are all the more necessary since rival conceptions of professional social work may compete for our allegiance.

Further, such items include more than certain forms of relation among professional social workers: certain forms of relation with clients are necessary. I said earlier that given a conception of professional social work implying use of relatively inaccessible skills and knowledge, a code of ethics had a part to play in the protection of clients. Add to this competing conceptions of professional social work, and the importance of certain forms of practice is emphasised. If the inaccessibility of the skills and knowledge in question is to be kept to a minimum, and also if the client is to have some prospect of choosing a relationship with a worker committed to principles and purposes he shares, then certain forms of practice must be the rule: in all cases the client should have the right to know the grounds upon which decisions have been taken, to present his case personally or through a representative, to question any disputed facts, and to appeal against the decision (see Barclay, 12.41).

These points seem to be recognised, at the usual rather abstract level, by Principles of Practice numbers 4 to 7. Principle 12 also reminds us, all too fleetingly, that the relation between professional and employer is crucial to good practice.

Even so, misconduct and incompetence will arise (see Barclay, para. 12.15). Who is to judge when it has arisen? The Code places that responsibility most heavily upon the social worker himself (see Principles of Practice, para. 10.7), but also upon the client (Commentary, On Principles, para. 11), and, more plausibly in view of clients' relative powerlessness, upon the professional association itself (Foreword, para. 5). Barclay reports BASW as supporting the idea of a General Social Work Council, amongst other things to clarify 'the question of what constitutes unprofessional conduct', and to help 'to define a reasonable standard of practice' (para. 12.21). Other proposals include 'an independent inspectorate which would monitor the practice of both social workers and their employing agencies' (para. 12.39), and 'local welfare advisory committees' (para. 12.60). So far as it is made clear, in every case the presumption is that practice is best judged by *fellow professional* social workers, even if they may seek the views of others. And yet judges of unprofessional practice are regularly described as *independent*.

They may in some sense be independent of the social worker whose practice is in question, but still share his conception of professional social work, and the principles and purposes implicit in it. In that case, though they might detect a failure to put the conception into practice, they will be quite unable to cope with complaints arising from a different view of what principles should be followed, or purposes pursued, in professional social work. These matters are not ones properly resolved internally by the social work profession, though it is widely *presumed* so. It is said that 'assessing need is a problematic activity at the best of times, but is one in which social workers are experienced and for which social work students are trained' (Barclay, para. 3.53, and see para. 10.5): professional social workers are the experts. In monitoring the performance of professional social workers the only question is 'the degree to which their allocation of resources corresponds to need' (para. 11.56); what is needed, as far as the experts are concerned, is unproblematic. Again, it is said that social workers have 'a distinctive clientele with a particular set of needs' (Pinker, in Barclay, p. 238), which can, no doubt, be readily identified.

Expertise in matters of need would warrant professional social workers being recognised as authoritative on the principles and purposes to be pursued in professional social work, intended to meet need. However, the presumption is mistaken; it is based on a misconception of the nature of need. As I argued at more length in my introduction to this book, what someone needs *is* a factual question, but it can be answered only by reference to some state of affairs or standard of future behaviour thought to be desirable: when people implementing policies identify what someone needs, they pick out what is in fact a means to a state or standard which the person identifying the lack believes *ought* to be brought about. That some present state or standard is undesirable, and that another is desirable, is not a matter determined by the use of the professional's distinctive skills or knowledge, but calls for an evaluative, and usually a moral, judgment.

I do not deny the importance of experience to evaluative judgment in some cases, but I do say that this kind of judgment is required in identifying need to be met, and that it is not the prerogative of any professional group in virtue of their expertise. And so also I do not suggest we abandon the idea of professional expertise: judgments of another kind also figure in the identification of need. Professional expertise lies in knowledge of what may reasonably be expected to have led to present circumstances, or to lead from them to particular objectives – knowledge of what may be expected to come about *if* (at para. 10.29 Barclay loses nerve). Professionals will no doubt continue to describe their knowledge of means as knowledge of needs to be met because in general they and their professional associations also take up evaluative positions on what present circumstances are undesirable and what final outcomes are desirable for their clients. These are implicit in their normative conceptions of the work of the profession, and to some extent, as we have seen, exposed in codes of ethics. But such positions are not themselves within the scope of their expertise.

For that reason, questions about the principles to be followed, and purposes pursued, in professional social work may not be ones appropriately settled in practice by General Social Work Councils, inspectorates, or local welfare advisory committees, if professional social worker members are their effective decision-makers. These are matters for *evaluative* judgment, to be settled by those to whom responsibility is allocated within a normative political theory. Such a theory identifies and argues for a view of the appropriate vehicle for control. Within *liberal* political theory what must above all be controlled is infringement of every person's equal right to be free (Hart, 1967). The responsibility for decision-making falls to *citizens*, though it may be delegated by them. Of course, decision-makers must seek the advice of any professionals about obstacles to practice of the principles and purposes which are authorised, but responsibility, to judge that the social worker has pursued those purposes *with reasonable care*, rests with them.

Further, wherever that responsibility lies, 'reasonable care' remains an expression in a public language in which standards for its correct use in particular types of context are established. However closely those sitting in judgment try to apply those standards, they inevitably apply them in a changing social environment in which it is always open to someone to argue that their judgment is mistaken, and so in this case unjust. Even though we must have decision-makers to settle questions about whether the principles and purposes of professional social work have been put into practice with reasonable care, and our political theory assigns that responsibility to lay people, what reasonable care *is* is not determined conclusively by any decision-making body. Like a conception of professional social work, it has a life of its own within a linguistic community of which professional social workers, or any lay decision-makers, can be *only* prominent members.

3

Summary of Part Two

I argued that the Code reaches a satisfactory level of specificity, from the point of view of the protection of clients, when supplemented either by material providing opportunities for self-criticism or by closer definition of the professional task in legislation or contracts of employment. Neither eliminates all need for professional discretion nor all unprofessional use of it. In such cases, where adjudication is necessary, and because the identification of need to be met presupposes evaluative judgment, within liberal political theory the responsibility rests with those by whom professional social workers are authorised in the first place to intervene in the lives of citizens: the citizens themselves.

2 Social work: what kind of profession?

Ruth Wilkes

In social work education and practice, the use of the word 'generic' has become another word for 'muddled'. It has been interpreted to mean that social workers must be taught as much as possible about every aspect of the work and, once qualified, they can be expected to turn their hands to practically anything required of them by their employers. Formerly a social worker trained in child care work or in medical psychiatric social work could reasonably be expected to be competent in these subjects and to be suited for their work since it had been their choice. The present hurry to produce competent experts in all fields has led to all manner of subjects being crammed into the curriculum and these are laid before students who may not have the education, the experience or the critical judgment to deal with them. Once qualified, matching the worker to the work may take second place to meeting what are thought to be the needs of the department. Those who, for whatever reason, do not enjoy the company of young children may, nevertheless, be expected to spend their working time dealing with non-accidental injury work or other activities with children; a social worker who has scarcely set foot in a residential home may be called upon to supervise the work of those who have given their lives to residential care; and a social worker with a special interest and aptitude for health care work may find himself or herself stimulating old people by helping them to pot hyacinth bulbs or to throw bean bags into buckets. All these activities can be included under the blanket term 'generic social work' and a qualified social worker available for such work is at risk of finding himself obliged to undertake it. It would be very surprising if this state of confusion did not give rise to merriment among the critics of social work and despair amongst its admirers.

Lurking at the back of this comical state of affairs lie two major unquestioned assumptions. In the first place action and study, living and learning are thought to be necessarily separate from each other. Theory, it is thought, does no more than leaven the lump and gives the profession a vitality it would not otherwise have, but from a practical point of view the really useful people are those who roll up their sleeves and get on with some specific task. In fact it is irrational to suppose that those who have a cultural background in the sense that they have studied excellence in the arts and sciences are less likely to be capable of right action than those who have given no thought to what they do. On the contrary, study, observation and reflection are a necessary prerequisite for right action if consideration is to be given to the remote consequences and possible side effects of some course of action. To avoid the harm that thought and patience might prevent, social workers need time for reflection and the opportunity to practice it. Without theory, in the sense of a creative vision which raises us above the practical level of everyday life, social work would be in danger of becoming a technological pursuit and the social worker no more than a technician carrying a capacious tool bag.

The second unquestioned assumption is the idea that there is some kind of specific social work expertise that makes the social worker *per se* better equipped than others to deal with the problems of life in any setting. Once in this position it becomes permissible for the social worker to set himself up as a counsellor to anyone. This way of thinking enables Patricia Morgan to write with some point about 'The care racket' (*Daily Telegraph*, 7 and 19 January 1983), and gives June Lait the opportunity to take a well aimed swipe at social work education, which she believes to be a 'spurious activity' because social workers do not have real expertise. (*Daily Telegraph*, 11 January 1983). For Mrs Lait, the work done by social workers would be better left to good neighbours and genuine carers and others possessing common-sense and concern. Unfortunately it is not as easy as that. In fact it is just because there is no social work expertise, in the sense that no one can be an expert where his neighbour is concerned, that education is necessary. Without the recognition that expertise in human relations is not the prerogative of any particular profession, social work deteriorates into an ideological pursuit, dedicated to the furtherance of some cause rather than to helping people to sort out their own plans in their own way. Social workers are already beginning to think of themselves as 'enablers' rather than as helpers, in the sense of encouraging clients to achieve independence by their own efforts. There is an implication that there is something wrong about being on the receiving end of care and attention; helplessness is equated with degradation and very much resented. This attitude is commonplace and is particularly noticeable in our treatment of the elderly. Old people are exhorted to take up new interests and to keep themselves busy, and success in retirement is measured by the extent to which the old person can truthfully say that he is so busy he wonders how he ever had time to go to work. This stereotype may be rubbed in by social workers who also like to be achievers and show that they are not standing idly by but are 'doing something'. For example, an old man spends his days sitting by the fire while his wife waits on him. An energetic social worker, thinking he should do more for himself, encourages him to do the washing-up by rewarding him, in behaviouristic fashion, with a packet of cigarettes whenever he achieves his allotted task. This endeavour comes to an end when the old man's wife complains that he is not himself and she liked it better when she was doing things for him. He liked receiving and she wanted to provide for him. It is to be hoped that the social worker recognises that enabling someone to do things for himself is not always appropriate.

The reluctance to accept and recognise the value of passivity leads to some disturbing policy changes in that priority is being given to those who can be 'enabled' at the expense of those who are dependent on the care and attention of others. The need for a non-ideological way of thinking was once stressed by Mother Teresa of Calcutta when she denied being a social worker because 'social workers work for a cause; the Church works for people'.

What is ideology and how does it relate to the values of social work? The word ideology has a history of ambiguity and its meaning is still not entirely clear. According to Aiken (1956, p. 16) the word was coined by a French philosopher, Destutt de Tracy (1754–1836) to refer to a radically empirical analysis of the human mind, claiming sense experience to be the origin of all ideas. This analysis was accepted by thinkers of the Enlightenment and became a way of thinking that could be expressed in political movements. The word thus denotes a philosophical theory about the knowledge of phenomena and also a system of attitudes and beliefs. For the thinkers of the Enlightenment empirical science was seen as the cure-all for the world's ills, but the emphasis put on subjective moral experience since the time of Kant (1724–1804) brought about a differentiation between ideology and the findings of empirical science. The influence of Marx (1818–1883) stressed the importance of changing the world and Marxist conceptions of ideology came to be seen as expressions of human relationships that were rooted in economic forces and social class. According to Aiken, Marx and Engels tried to distinguish between the ideological components of consciousness and what they refer to as real positive science. Marx thought of his own theories as scientific and empirically based, but events proved his predictions to be largely mistaken. Unfortunately, his followers found it difficult to admit that Marx's theories were not scientific and have adopted an attitude of commitment to the establishment of a free and equal society in spite of empirical evidence, not available to Marx, strongly indicating that the existence of a communist society requires a degree of co-operation only obtained in a coercive society. The ideologue who thinks in terms of putting ideas into practice sees himself to be subjectively right, but he also has the moral fervour of the evangelist because he knows his cause is just and, furthermore, he speaks not only for himself but on behalf of like-minded people. Aiken (1958, p. 157), in an essay in which he is concerned 'to distinguish morality as such from ideology as such in the interests of both', sees the ideologue as someone who is always partisan and committed to an objectivism that precludes reconsideration and sober thought. The ideologue has a closed mind in the sense that there is no vertical self-criticism, nothing outside his system of ideas that might give him pause, or cause him to think it possible that he may be wrong. In this sense of the word, ideology can be used as a weapon and an expression of the will-to-power.

Disagreement is not tolerated because it either confirms the theory held by the ideologue, as in the case of marxists or Freudians, or the evidence offered does not fit the favoured theory and therefore cannot be accepted, as in the case of behaviourism. In contrast the moral agent, according to Aiken (1958, p. 164) represents a point of view which is essentially personal. The moral agent is a man of conscience with a sense of personal guilt and personal responsibility for his conduct towards others. 'Moral freedom is not the freedom to do as you please but the freedom to decide what sort of person you ought to be' (Aiken, 1958, p. 159). This decision is subjective and is not imposed on the subject by authority of any kind. As Kant put it morality is a law you impose on yourself. The authority for morality is ultimately internal, never external. The Socratic dialogue of the soul with itself is never closed, and often judgment must be reserved. 'In short,' writes Aiken (1958, p. 168), '[it is] the orthodoxy of the ideologue; not the principles which the orthodoxy adheres to, which the moralist must resent.'

This distinction between the moral agent, or the man of conscience, and the ideologue is, perhaps, the philosophical justification for Mother Teresa's distinction between working for a cause and working for a person, and it is of the utmost relevance to social work theory and practice. Ideologies come and go, an individual can accept different ideologies at different times or no ideology at any time, but respect for the individual is a constant categorical imperative. This is not to say that the ideologue may not, on occasions, be right, but he needs to be watched lest the individual is to be sacrificed for the good of the cause. The cause is usually seen as some greater whole of which the individual is a small and insignificant part. From the point of view of the individual who is struggling to realise himself, it does not matter whether this greater whole is the 'community' as it is for the marxist, or the 'department' or the 'service' as it is for the manager. In either case the individual is only respected if he holds the right opinions or does, or can be forced to do, the right things.

The protection of the individual's right to decide for himself what sort of person he or she ought to be is an essential function of a code of ethics. Within the humane and liberal tradition of western culture the central concept of morality is the individual and the value put upon him. The conception of human life expressed in the New Testament has its counterpart in testimonies from other civilisations. C. S. Lewis has collected an impressive variety of quotations from many sources and countries to illustrate an arguable thesis that 'every civilisation we find has derived from another civilisation and, in the last resort, from a single centre – 'carried' like an infectious disease or like the Apostolical succession' (1943, p. 48). Whether Europe was ever truly Christianised in the sense of practising the Gospel conception of life is debatable, and certainly the evidence of the Inquisition and the testament of heretics indicates that conversion was often to an ideology of submission to the authority of the Church. Since the Renaissance the spirit of scientific enquiry and the search for truth, which should have been liberating influences, have been seen in the light of the domination and conquest of nature, and the idea of uniqueness has become an individualism that can be equated with doing as you please, or what Matthew Arnold, commenting on an absence of sweetness and light in Victorian times, called 'the heaven-born privilege of the Populace . . . marching where it likes, meeting where it likes, bawling what it likes, breaking what it likes' (1970, p. 254). This kind of individualism is particularly dangerous when set against a cultural background which Arnold described as philistinism; that is the preference for action over thinking, for energy over intelligence. Arnold looked to culture, 'which simply means trying to perfect oneself', and the principle of right reason to counteract the tendency to anarchy which seemed to be threatening his society (1970, pp. 235–6). Unfortunately the anarchists in our midst are likely to feel for their guns when they hear the word 'culture'.

The importance of a code of ethics lies in the provision of a standard against which the actions of a profession can be judged, and puts constraints both on the power of the established ideology to dominate and control the individual and on the inclination of the unrestrained individual to do as he pleases. The BASW Code of Ethics attempts to express these requirements.

The BASW Code of Ethics stresses the law of general beneficence – of never doing to others what you would not like them to do to you – in its Statement of Principles designed to respect human value and dignity: 'to ensure the fullest possible realisation of [the client's] rights and satisfaction of his needs' and to recognise 'the value and dignity of every human being, irrespective of origin, status, sex, sexual orientation, age, belief or contribution to society'. It accepts a responsibility 'to encourage and facilitate the self-realisation of the individual person with due regard to others.' This view implies that there is something uniquely valuable in every human being and that what constrains me in my dealing with another is the thought that I may do him harm. For Kant the moral principle that man is an end in himself who cannot, and should not, be treated simply as a means, presents itself to us as a categorical imperative which we perceive as a principle we are bound to follow regardless of inclination, and without making exceptions in favour of ourselves. Furthermore, the principle is accepted for its own sake, unlike a hypothetical imperative which tells us what we must do to achieve a certain end; for example, I must leave London by an early train if I wish to be in Edinburgh by tea time. It is important to note that respect for the individual as an unique being refers to every individual as a human being for what he is and not by virtue of what he possesses by way of intelligence, power, status or anything else. Fromm makes a distinction between two basic modes of existence, the mode of being and the mode of having (1979, p. 29). The having orientation is centred around things, and the being orientation is centred around persons; in the having mode my relationship to the world is one of possessing and owning, in the being mode my relationships leave the other person free to grow nearer to the goal of becoming himself, in the spirit of the Tao Te Ching:

> I take no action and the people are transformed of themselves: I prefer stillness and the people are rectified of themselves: I am not meddlesome and the people prosper of themselves: I am free from desire and the people of themselves become simple like the uncarved block. (Lao Tzu, 1963, p. 118)

It is the essence of a person considered as an 'uncarved block' that he is allowed to grow in accordance with his own nature untouched by the interference of human ingenuity. For this to happen the individual needs space to grow, freedom to develop and warmth for the soul to germinate. These are conditions normally denied to us by modern societies in which, Fromm says, 'the growing person is forced to give up most of his or her autonomous will, and to adopt a will and desires and feelings that are not autonomous but superimposed by the social patterns of thought and feeling' (1979, p. 83). Simone Weil makes a similar point when she writes of the modern factory that 'everybody in it is constantly harassed and kept on edge by the interference of extraneous wills while the soul is left in cold and desolate misery: what man needs is silence and warmth; what he is given is an icy pandemonium' (1962, p. 17).

The notion of respect for the individual extends to all human beings irrespective of their achievements, or lack of them. Infants and the immature are not normally treated as objects to be controlled and humiliated by others but what of the severely mentally retarded? Distinctions need to be made between individual human beings and persons. It is sometimes thought that what is of value in a human being is something called his 'person' or 'personality'. Simone Weil dismisses this thought as a grave error because it is possible to respect a personality but degrade the individual concerned. 'If it were human personality in him that was sacred to me, I could easily put out his eyes. As a blind man he would be exactly as much a human personality as before. I should not have touched the person in him at all. I should have destroyed nothing but his eyes' (1962, p. 9). She adds that people who feel something sacred in their own persons do so 'if they feel it in respect of their own person . . . but it participates in collective prestige through the social consideration bestowed upon it' (pp. 40–1). Downie and Telfer make a distinction between the subnormal and the normal human being by employing the evaluative concept of a *person* to mark off those human beings who are worthy of full respect for the individual and they imply that the senile, the severely mentally ill and infants are not really persons, and are not therefore worthy of full respect. They must, however, be treated better than animals because of their kinship with *persons* who are of the same species (Downie and Telfer, 1980, p. 38).

Watson considers respect for human beings is a logically possible alternative to respect for persons because 'active sympathy', one of the components of respect, 'may be directed towards human beings who are not 'persons' in the full sense, but who nevertheless may have ends at which 'someone might reasonably be expected to aim even if he is in fact unable to choose these aims for himself, formulate purposes, plans and policies of his own, or govern his conduct by rules'. Watson concludes that respect for human beings is the most fundamental principle because it aims to encourage and develop such capacities as 'the capacities to be emotionally secure, to receive love and affection, and to be content and free from worry' (Watson, 1978, pp. 44–6). These capacities are generally possessed by children and the senile, and furthermore this kind of respect for human beings is 'the most general principle of action entailed by the attitude of compassion represented by social work' (p. 48).

Perhaps the point has been laboured; it might be simpler and more accurate to say with Simone Weil, 'It is neither his person, nor the human personality in him, which is sacred to be. It is he. The whole of him. The arms, legs, the thoughts, everything. Not without infinite scruple would I touch anything of this' (1962,

p. 11). On this argument no one is expendable and all are worthy of respect.

The question of what is meant by self-realisation is difficult to answer if it is thought of in terms of what people do, are capable of doing, or can be made to do; or is seen in the light of worldly success and adjustment to the opinions and wishes of others, except in so far as these opinions and wishes can be identified with the interest of the individual concerned. The idea that self-realisation means social adjustment is open to question on the grounds that it involves self-surrender or self-sacrifice, even to the extent that may lead the true believer to think he has nothing to live for unless he is ready to die for it. Such fanaticism forms the basis for mass movements and although it may be argued that movements of this kind may be beneficial – the Reformation and some revolutions and nationalist movements – the capacity of the individual to resist coercion and to stand out against the mass may be reduced to nil. Techniques of persuasion may make the individual agree to be moulded nearer to someone else's heart's desire, although, in his quieter, more reflective moments, he might have seen things differently.

Equally open to question is the notion that, provided it is not anti-social or illegal, all an individual's capacities should be realised to their fullest extent without discrimination. Nielson (1976, p. 116) emphasises the dilettante aspect of this idea of self-realisation and points out that since man has many different powers and he cannot develop them all, particularly when they conflict, 'it is not clear what he is to do to realise his own nature' (p. 123). Reference may be made to our 'highest and best capacities', but who is to decide what these are or how they should be realised? Appeals to reason do not help because the ancient view of man as a bearer of reason linking him to all created things has been vulgarised into a concept of analytic reason that destroys the whole by breaking things down into their component parts by means of observation and calculation, without trying to make anything constructive out of it. We collect data, diagnose and assess on the basis of what is positively presented to us, but we do not attempt to see the whole picture or go beyond the theoretical explanation. We are left not with the whole man – body, mind and spirit – but with the parts we can observe and measure; any reference to the wonder of creation or to the essential nature of man is ruled out on principle.

Furthermore the emphasis on reason makes those of weak minds open to the accusation that they are, as Aristotle thought, 'slaves of nature' because they are incapable of self-direction and therefore not human beings.

Linking self-realisation to ideas of happiness fares no better under scrutiny. There are differences as well as similarities among individuals and it cannot be assumed that what satisfies one will satisfy another, and in any event happiness is a will-o'-the-wisp that proves elusive when pursued. The moral ideal of the greatest happiness of the greatest number is defensible when considered in the light of basic necessities common to all but is hard to defend when considered in the light of good and evil. Iris Murdoch observes that we must be very corrupted by philosophy if we cannot see that some things are better than others. For example, great art can be distinguished from trash, and humble people who serve others are commonly thought to be better than the selfish and arrogant. It does not follow, however, that good art gives more happiness than bad art or that humble people are happier than arrogant people. On the contrary if life is reduced to the condition involved in doing what pleases us it is unlikely that most of us will pursue what is good, since excellence in the arts and unselfishness in conduct may be painful. For this reason those who achieve happiness through ambition, greed, cruelty, etc. are more numerous than those whose happiness comes from the willingness to put themselves out for others and to meet suffering and affliction for the sake of acting well. It was said by the Stoics that a good man can be happy on the rack, but this other-worldly concept of happiness is not accepted by most people.

Human beings are sufficiently self-assertive to claim the right to happiness of some kind, but the need to treat each other as unique individuals worthy of consideration as ends in themselves needs to be constantly re-asserted. It is a command that proves difficult to put into practice. Probably this is because there is a mysteriousness that adheres to the self. It is a mystery because it cannot be singled out as a separate entity existing apart from the individual and it cannot be defined. In a sense it does not exist and self-knowledge and self-realisation are delusions. It is however important to consider each individual as a separate self, unique and different from all others, because it is this recognition that provides the distance between individuals required to enable each solitary one to live in accordance with his nature. As Iris Murdoch puts it: 'The more the separateness and differences of other people is realised, and the fact seen that another man has needs and wishes as demanding as one's own, the harder it becomes to treat a person as a thing' (1970, p. 66).

The BASW Code of Ethics recognises 'the value and dignity of every human being' and accepts 'the responsibility to encourage and facilitate the self-realisation of the individual person with due regard to others'. At the same time social work education teaches methods that are decidedly directive in that they are based on theories purporting to explain human behaviour with a view to improving it. People are often thought to be mouldable, or at least directable, by practitioners who see the clients as part of their treatment plan. As Goldstein put it: 'practice theories in particular are typically directive in so far as they outlined sets of strategies or principles that ought to be followed so as to achieve a successful interview, proper data collection, a helpful relationship, and so on. In this regard, such theories are uni-directional: they point to what the helper needs to do to or with clients' (in an unpublished essay, from which I have the author's permission to quote). The social worker is in charge and his methods seek to control. Far from being helped to 'follow his own nature' and work out his own problems in his own way the client is expected to fit someone else's pattern and sacrifice himself to some ideology designed to change him for the better.

When this happens it would be more honest to say that by self-realisation we mean self-sacrifice. The underlying value judgment of much social work thinking and practice is that a human being, far from being an end in himself, can and should be changed or made to adjust to some social norm. It is not just that there is no suggestion that changing people is wrong: there is no acknowledgment of the view that changing people amounts to a mutilation of the self because there is a sacred core in every man that can only be touched at the cost of doing infinite harm to him. If you want to influence others you do not do it by techniques of manipulation or by issuing instructions. You must, as Marx says:

> be a person who really has a stimulating and encouraging effect upon others. Every one of your relations to man and to nature must be a *specific expression*, corresponding to the object of

your will, of your *real individual* life. If you love without evoking love in return, i.e. if you are not able, by the *manifestation* of yourself as a loving person, to make yourself a beloved person, then your love is impotent and a misfortune.
(Quoted, as translated by Fromm, in Fromm, 1979, pp. 155–6)

The kind of approach that invites others to respond in a spirit of trust is not encouraged by social workers who have identified a target and worked out a strategy for hitting it. Spontaneity is replaced by conscious decision-making and we are 'helped' by being told not to be what we are but to decide to be something else. The client is expected to decide to stop beating his children or to speak to his wife at least twice a week, or whatever behaviour is considered to be socially acceptable. Unfortunately for the sim- plicity of this approach real decisions are never made in this way. Like mountain scenery the best decisions unfold as you go along. Tell yourself that from now on you intend to be charitable or humble and you will find that everyone prudently moves as far away from you as possible because your good will is overpowering, or you will be no more than Uriah Heep or what Blake once called a 'petty sneaking knave'. This is because the decision is superficial and does not go deep enough to discover the malice and aggressiveness that lurks within the dark recesses of the mind. Such discoveries are private and do not form part of the data social workers are taught to collect. In this way we easily mistake the artificial world with its superficial warmth for the real world of the solitary individual. The real culprit here is behaviourism with its basic assumption of a model that eliminates the self as a substantial entity. 'Man is above all an adaptive, learning animal,' writes Sheldon. 'Institutions and organisations devised by him have the primary functioning of controlling behaviour for special purposes' (Sheldon, 1978, p. 53). If the ends of morality and the organisation do not coincide, this is thought to be due to some failure of communication and the behaviour of the erring individual must be controlled in the interests of the special purposes held to be important by authority. The behavioural approach is surprisingly managerial in that in each case the unwanted self is easily disposed of for the sake of some adaptation to a cause. In behaviouristic psychology the cause is the achievement of what is thought to be desirable behaviour, while those committed to the managerial ideology of 'belongingness' sacrifice themselves and others to the institution or the organisation. Respect for the individual and the concept of self-realisation are apt to be brushed aside by these rather bracing approaches. Indeed the present emphasis in social work thought and practice on 'integration', 'team work', and on various kinds of behavioural therapies seem to have more to do with the imposition of conformity than with prevention or alleviation of individual distress and suffering, and very little to do with the growth of self-knowledge seen in the light of 'being myself' as the goal of living.

The principle of respect for individuals applies to colleagues as well as to clients. Managers and workers alike forget at their peril that people are not robots but human beings who need to be treated with respect if the workplace is not to become stiff with friction and mistrust leading to wasteful industrial strife. The need is for good human relations in industry but what is provided is management of personnel by the bureaucratic method. Fromm defines this method:

> as one that (a) administers human beings as if they were things and (b) administers things in quantitative rather than qualitative terms, in order to make quantification and control easier and cheaper. The bureaucrats base their decisions on fixed rules arrived at from statistical data, rather than on *response to the living beings who stand before them*: they decide issues according to what is statistically most likely to be the case, at the risk of hurting five or ten per cent of those who do not fit into that pattern (1979, p. 181).

Instead of trying to provide the conditions in which workers can participate and be truly active in their roles, the bureaucratic way of thinking seeks refuge behind rules that remove personal responsibility from the worker and treats him or her as an object to be used, a unit of production or part of a workforce to be 'prioritised'. This method is authoritarian and expresses the bullying 'I am in charge do as I tell you' mentality. The worker loses all faculty for critical thinking and indeed criticism is resented and interpreted as insubordination or trouble-making to be stamped out by appeals to loyalty, attacks on attitudes and dissenting opinions, monitoring and various forms of disciplinary action. Loyalty to rules makes it possible for managers to turn on to automatic pilot and leave their offices to run themselves in accordance with rules and procedures laid down from the top. The office is seen as an efficiently working machine and workers become mechanics, or at least sheep. Once the rules have been laid down and the workers trained to carry out instructions 'even a person of mediocre intelligence and ability can easily run a state once he or she is in the seat of power' (Fromm, 1979, p. 180). When this kind of bureaucratic management operates in an organisation employing social workers where both managers and practitioners are qualified social workers, it is doubly unfortunate because it leads to a split profession. The managers operate as expert officials owing their primary loyalty to their employers, while the practitioners operate as professional social workers owing their primary loyalty to their clients. Malcolm Payne elsewhere in this book illustrates what can happen in disputes between clients and doctors; senior managers in an agency support the doctors' sides against what social workers take to be the interests of the clients, 'arguing that the maintenance of co-operation was more important for the generality of clients than the interests of these particular clients'.

The mistake of bureaucratic management is to think that the procedures of management of commodities and physical objects can be transferred with a minimum of modification to working with human beings. There is, as Dilthey points out in his philosophy of history (see Hodges, 1944), a difference between our knowledge of minds and our knowledge of physical things. In a sense we can know physical nature with more certainty than we can know man and society, but knowledge of things lacks the sympathetic insight which enables one person to appreciate the motives and meaning of actions for another. It is this sympathy and feeling of identity of nature between ourselves and other human beings that is absent in the idea of bureaucratic management. The result is a great unwillingness to tolerate differences and to recognise that a diversity of views is a criticism of ideas and experiences, and not an attack on good will or motivation.

It is not necessary for a human being in a bureaucratic position to behave in a bureaucratic way; he can adopt a humanistic method of management. Humanistic management asks for the active partici-pation of those who are 'managed' and seeks independent views in the Socratic spirit of following the evidence and the argument 'whithersoever it may lead'. In an occupation claiming to be a profession this means living with the uncertainty of having to make independent judgments that may turn out to be wrong.

To what extent can social work be thought of as a profession and how should professional people be regarded? Lewis and Maude, in their study of professional people, state three separate views. First, there is the tradesman view of professional people as people who have special skills, 'more elaborate than, but not different in kind from, the skills of lathe-setters and draughtsmen'. Alternatively they may be seen as officials, or even, in some cases, super-officials, 'using their techniques to modify the conduct, and experiment with the reactions, of the salariat and the proletariat'. Third, they are 'the guardians of a tradition, humane and Christian, of study and service to their fellows, whether this is based on a confidential and fiduciary relationship with individual clients or on voluntary sacrifice of extra monetary gain in the interests of the community' (Lewis and Maude, 1952, p. 10). The BASW Code of Ethics emphasises the importance of humane principles even to the point of recognising that in certain circumstances a social worker may have to resign his post, if he or she is asked to break a fundamental principle. There is no suggestion that a social worker is simply an expert official implementing policies laid down by his political masters. This is not to say that it is not important for social workers to co-operate with their employers, but there is a world of difference between co-operation and subservience. The employment of social workers in the public service is a danger area unless professional workers set their own standards and claim the right to make independent professional judgments. It cannot be a matter of indifference to social workers what lay people think of their standards and judgments, but the final test of this is whether anyone can be found to employ them. It does not, however, follow that society, in the shape of the state or of employing authorities, is right if it disagrees with a profession's standards and judgments.

The failure of the medical profession to take an effective stand against the Nazis is a salutary warning to those who would have the piper play to his paymaster's bidding. But if the professional claims a degree of independence from his employer there is a need for a professional organisation to provide the disciplinary framework within which practitioners can function as well as to protect the practitioner from the threat of state bureaucracy which can become as tyrannical as any autocracy. Equally important is the need for professional education to establish standards and to safeguard the independence of the practitioner. The threat to education is another danger area unless there is clarity of thought concerning the nature of social work as a profession. The pragmatic, utilitarian approach of the tradesman view of professional people is impatient of theories and ideas, and leads to a practical kind of training emphasising flexibility. In practice this may mean the bending of principles and ideals to meet the demands of circumstances and the claims of expediency. However expert and high-minded officials may be, they are dependent on those who employ them unless it is recognised that they have an obligation to maintain professional values and standards of practice.

The present tension between education and training reflects Lewis and Maude's distinction between what are essentially two contrasting views of professional people; namely, the view that stresses the tradition of study and service to others, and the view that stresses the practical aspects of the work. The new CSS training, favoured by employers because of its job-related nature and flexibility, supports the view of the professional as a practical worker who can work under managerial instruction. According to a training officer who is enthusiastic about the CSS innovation, 'the planning and design of any CSS scheme always begins with a thorough and detailed analysis of the roles and tasks each worker is required to perform, the skills to be used, and the necessary feelings and attitudes associated with each task for its competent and effective performance' (Pragnell, 1983). The idea is to acquire knowledge required to perform specific tasks and to accompany the 'necessary feelings and attitudes'. It may be going too far to say with Professor Leonard that this kind of training involves the 'de-skilling of social workers', but it undoubtedly tilts the balance away from the traditional general, educational base of social work training towards a more severely practical and utilitarian approach, based on an apprenticeship form of occupational training.

The dilemma is not a new one. The professions have long been graded between those fit for gentlemen (the Church and the Army), and those that were practised by tradesmen (barbers, surgeons, dentists) or by mechanics (engineers). Historically social work has accommodated both the gentlemen and the tradesmen views, and this is reflected in the content and method of traditional training. The original social work training started by C. S. Loch and the Charity Organisation Society in 1899 was based on a course of general social science and students were not accepted unless they were at least 25 years of age. According to E. Moberly Bell, COS training was intended as something much more serious than equipping candidates for a job; the concern of the originators of social work training extended to helping the clergy and voluntary workers with a view to the enlightenment of public opinion. The importance of practical work was not underestimated. In order to obtain skills and techniques, 'Practical work was undertaken at Settlements and in the COS offices, where it was strongly insisted that the student was not to be used as an extra office boy, but made to study each case in relation to local conditions' (Bell, 1961, p. 91). The hospital almoning pioneers were so insistent on the value of experience that they would not accept the authority of the Administrative Council of the COS to determine the suitability of candidates to become almoners because they 'were unwilling to believe that a committee composed almost entirely of men who had no experience of the day to day work in an almoner's office, could be as capable of choosing the right woman as their own committee' (Bell, 1961, p. 47).

The 'gentlemen' concept of a professional person stresses the need for professional education and training to go beyond equipping students for the performance of specific tasks because general culture, considered as a study of perfection, sets limits to what Arnold calls 'the unrestrained swing of the individual's personality, our maxim of "every man for himself" ' (1970, p. 209). The cultivated mind tries to see more than one point of view and avoids the inflexibility that arises from total absorption in the performance of whatever particular pursuit we happen to be following. Culture today finds the going hard partly because the idea of a gentleman is considered to be old-fashioned, if not elitist. There is however, a perennial definition of a gentleman, stated by Cardinal Newman, as one who never inflicts pain. It is the requirement to avoid doing harm to others that makes the general culture of the mind the best foundation for professional study. It enables us to reflect on the nature of our practice and to consider the effects of our actions on others. It is a philosophic habit of mind that actively seeks the views and considers the interests of others and comes to conclusions only after genuine discussion with all those concerned and after give and take on all sides. In a word, tolerance replaces conflict or consensus as the proper mode of discourse.

There is much to be learned from the precepts and practice of the pioneers of social work education. Before any giant steps are taken in the wrong direction it would be as well to reconsider the recommendations of the Younghusband Report on Social Workers in the Local Authority Health and Welfare Services (1959). This report distinguishes between university-based training for the highest social work qualification; a general training to be given in colleges of further education or other educational establishments, with the co-operation of the universities, leading to a national qualification sufficient for certain appointments and for promotion within the appropriate local authority grading; and planned in-service training for welfare assistants. In the event, the first two qualifications have been absorbed into one CQSW training and the present debate on course qualification contains the view that the level and status of qualifications gained should not be a reflection of the level of the educational establishment. In the interests of egalitarianism, particularly in relation to conditions of service and to salary scales, it seems to be suggested that a training course based at the Little Twittering School of Catering, Stitchery and Lace should not be deemed to be at a disadvantage when placed alongside a degree course at Oxford University. In making the highest kind of social work professional education a task of the university, the Younghusband Report did not set out to tease those whose minds and hearts are set on whatever is down-to-earth and useful. It is stating the view that social work is a professional activity in the humane and liberal tradition, and not merely a practical job oriented to specific tasks.

The occupational training of specialists is important, but more important is the provision of a general education 'which gives a man a clear conscious view of his own opinions and judgements, a truth in developing them, an eloquence in expressing them, and a force in urging them' (Newman, 1947, p. 157). This is the idea of university training as expressed by Newman. It is 'the great ordinary means to a great but ordinary end'. Such an education is based on a sense of civilised values and should bestow on the student a habit of mind 'which lasts through life, of which the attributes are, freedom, equitableness, calmness, moderation and wisdom' (Newman, 1947, p. 90). The intellect is not sacrificed to some specific profession but is trained to a vision of greatness that enables the student to discriminate between the first-rate and the shoddy, the true and the false. The need to discover values, to question the assumptions that underly our reasoning and to have some philosophical understanding of external movements and changes is an urgent and neglected task, and one that is emphatically useful.

A professional education is vitally important for the establishment and maintenance of a concern for, but not necessarily agreement on, values and standards of practice, and this education must exist independently of the employing authority. In 1952 Lewis and Maude wrote: 'The moment that the state organises, trains and employs all the members of a profession, we can no longer speak of it as a profession. We can only speak of a body of expert officials.' If the general education of the mind, which is the hallmark of a liberal university education, is ever sacrificed to job-oriented training, this moment will have arrived.

3 Personal and professional values – marriage or divorce?

Neil Leighton

Part One

Social workers are people as well as social workers, and have personal views of the social world and the way they feel it ought to be. Only some of those personal views will be reflected in assertions about what social workers' views should be. The presumption that some personal views will, or should, be shared by some other social workers, or in a code of ethics by *all* other social workers, needs examination. Social workers tend to take for granted that professional views will generally coincide with personal views. There are, however, discrepancies which need to be fully recognised. For example, a social worker may expect his general view of how people should relate to each other to be reflected in his professional values; turning the other cheek in reaction to anger or abuse will be common to his personal and professional world. Suppose however that in his personal life he adopts an attitude to his social world framed upon a homosexual orientation. Surely he should not press that framework upon other social workers and he will not assert the pattern as one which can be promoted for all clients. This chapter will emphasise the need to map out the territory of shared presumptions before asserting a social work ethic.

Discussion of the BASW Code of Ethics cannot embrace moral issues raised by helping in general or the promotion of altruism. The focus is upon a code of professional practice to be adopted by all those engaged in social work as a professional activity.

The Code commences with the words 'social work is a professional activity'. Nowhere does it elaborate upon what it means by 'social work' nor does it list those activities which are included or excluded from the description 'professional social work'. This must give cause for concern because some of the boundaries to the social work activities have fundamental impact on the ethical principles. For example, community and group work must adopt a very different standard of confidentiality from private clinical psychotherapy. David Watson and Huw Richards take up discussion of this limitation elsewhere in this volume.

It is very understandable that the code avoids defining social work. The Barclay Report (Barclay, 1982), was prepared by a team whose primary task was the description and definition of what social work is but as they advanced beyond the traditional 'therapeutic' task of personal work with individual clients, they invaded the activities often or even usually carried out by people who are not professional social workers. Their inclusion of 'social care planning' (para. 3.35) as a social work activity is undermined by their admission in the same paragraph that most parents also undertake social care planning for their family. Is this social care planning social work? Or is it only social work when it is done by a 'social worker'? How can we avoid the apparently endless debate in seeking to define social work? In the absence of a proper definition of the activity of social work, how can the discussion of the ethics move forward?

The Code discussion paper stated that the Working Party had tried to produce a code which will be generally applicable but goes on to say that whether the code is equally applicable to say, the child guidance worker, the community worker and the social work administrator is a matter for discussion. It would seem to be a fundamental principle that a code of ethics for a professional must be stated in such a form that it is binding upon all members of the profession, not more binding upon some than others. It seems that the Code declares that social work is simply what a professional social worker does. This delegates the responsibility of defining social work to the Membership Committee of the Association because it is they who will decide who may call himself a social worker within the professional Association.

The Association of Directors of Social Services in their document *The Role and Tasks of Social Workers: Evidence to the NISW Working Party* (1982) distinguished it simply as a form of 'a professional activity requiring additional knowledge and skills which only appropriate training can provide'. This is little more than saying that to be a professional requires training. The Directors, will, however, be very aware that they employ many people undertaking residential social work who have many of the professional skills although they are not qualified social workers.

These statements Medawar would find to be 'vague and barely articulate' (1982, p. 84). Following his method we might have something of the form. 'There is a wide but definable class of social situations into which a social worker is introduced in order to modify the social interaction.' We can then go further to state 'when the behaviour of the social worker is governed by expectations which reflect the collective views of social workers with regard to standards of practice, then it will be called professional social work'; 'a statement of Social Work Ethics is a distillation of the principles which the Associations of Social Workers regard as governing professional social work practice.'

There are two particularly important elements in the initial statement. One is the opportunity to list in a definitive way (Watson, in chapter 1 of this volume, offers some reason to think no list can be definitive) the situations which require action by a social worker as distinct from any other member of the community, family, friend or other professional. The other is that the introduction of the worker has a particular purpose – to modify the relationship between the client and their social environment. This latter point may touch a sensitive nerve because it unashamedly admits the manipulative use of relationships by the social worker. It is essential, however, that the difference between the personal relationships upon which the technique of relating is founded and professional relationships is identified because to confuse the two is risky for both clients and workers. An important value judgment is also entangled if these two modes of relationship are confused. In a professional relationship the purpose of assisting the client is *primary* and effectiveness should determine the choice of relationship to be entered into. In personal relationships the idea of *using* people, oneself or others, in the pursuit of some ulterior objective does not meet with the approval of idealists. It is done and we are often the proponents and also the victims, but many regard it as a matter for regret. This is at the core of the ethical difference between professional and personal relationships; one is purposive and the other is generally regarded as of a higher level or of a better quality if it is not.

Many clients are as aware as social workers of the difference between the relationship which the social worker forms whilst they are being a social worker and the relationships they form as private persons. This 'not being related as other people are' may be as necessary for the recipient of social work as it is for the workers. Social workers who have sought help with their own social difficulties or who have had their help sought by members of their family or neighbours become immediately aware of the importance of the 'protective' boundary which the professional relationship offers and the shattering effect it has if it is attempted in the context of personal relationships.

If the separation of the personal and professional is accepted, there is associated with it a difference of power or authority between the person who defines himself as the client and the person designated 'the therapist' or 'social worker'. If this is the chosen relationship pattern which enables the situation to be 'contained' in the most helpful way for both parties then it is not to be deplored. This calls into question the central presumptions of the BASW Discussion Paper *Clients are Fellow Citizens* (BASW, 1980). The aspect of 'personhood' which is a part of being a full citizen in forming intimate personal relationships has been voluntarily abandoned by those clients who have sought help just as it has been put aside by the person donning the role of social worker. Neither are then full fellow citizens in the professional relationship and it calls into question whether it is correct to assume or imply that they ought to be.

This acceptance of an inequality in the power relationship between 'therapist' and 'client' may be a source of differentiation between those aspects of social work which are 'service provision', and those aspects which involve the social worker in the interactions between the personality of the client, or his social contacts, and the world in which he or she lives. It is certainly a matter which social service managers have tended to 'fudge' and is not a differentiation of tasks about which the Barclay Report makes any clear statement, or which is faced in the BASW Code. The insidious presumption of the casework model applied to all aspects of social service provision is ever-present; the person with an amputated leg who seeks registration as a handicapped person may be required to be seen by a social worker, whether he requests it or not, whereas he may only feel he needs to give a description of his problem of functioning in order to get a bus pass. Is social *service* provision a right, and social work provision something which clients should be allowed to contract out of? Is there a different ethic for service provision than there is for social casework?

There is a further set of persons with whom a social caseworker may interact; those who do not come to the social worker for assistance at all, but come offering personal service or as relatives of a client. Is there a separate social work ethic to be applied to them?

The BASW Code is heavily oriented towards the one-to-one model of social casework practice and fails to give firm guidance to those faced with the conflicting obligations falling upon them within statutory agencies (as Payne argues in his contribution to this volume), or with task-oriented group work or community work as their social work method. Principle 6, for example, accepts 'a responsibility to encourage and facilitate the self-realisation of the individual person with due regard for the interests of others'. Does it help when applied to practical situations?

Consider the social worker who has responsibility to supervise the living situation of a 2-year-old child whose mother has inflicted cigarette burns on his abdomen and is also inclined to vent her anger in a more abandoned but less sadistic way by beating the child. As the case has been described the infant is obviously the social worker's 'primary' client; his interests must be the first consideration in the work plan. But he is young and inarticulate and therefore social work intervention must focus on the 'secondary' client, the mother. Without the application of a great amount of casuistry, what use can be made of the Code's guidance of encouraging and facilitating self-realisation for this mother? (See Nielsen, 1976.) The self which she is realising has a sadistic aspect and even that part of herself which is impulse-dominated cannot be more fully realised without increasing the risk to the infant. Indeed that impulse-ridden part must be subject to control, and the sadistic part of the self be subject to some kind of modification or transformation rather than realisation. This case underlines some of the presumptions which social workers make but which are rarely articulated: that there are forms of the self which are not in accord with social work goals; principle 6 is directed towards an unspoken ideal model of selfhood. One element of that selfhood may be to have due regard to the interests of others. We might press it further and ask whether that 'due regard' is that which is due under the criminal or civil law, or determined by some moral criterion. More detailed examination of notions such as the 'ideal self' is emerging in therapeutic models such as psychosynthesis, which avoids the focus on pathology common to most models of treatment and emphasises developmental ideals and personal moral choices (Assiglioni, 1974).

Furthermore, attempts to articulate a common view of selfhood reveal much wider differences than might be expected. For example in the case above we have a glimpse of a notion of motherhood as a form of selfhood, but the feminist and the male chauvinist will have very different views on the concept of motherhood and its relationship to the selfhood of women, and there will also be different views of the relationship between the state and the individual in the fulfilment of parenting roles. These parameters will set a framework within which the self of the mother in the case will or will not be moved towards 'self-realisation', and we may expect a different framework for different workers. Are the determinants of these choices personal or professional views?

We cannot therefore safely assume a common understanding of 'self-realisation' in principle 6. The same discrepancy of views may be evoked by principle 7, which declares that the profession attempts to relieve and prevent hardship and suffering. What is its impact on professional decision-making when counselling parents who have a physically and mentally handicapped child born to them, or who offer to look after someone else's handicapped child. Caring for such a child will often be a source of hardship and suffering which could be relieved most effectively by parting with the child. Some may say that in an imperfect world hardship and suffering are ever-present and that the quality of each life is reflected in the manner of our coming to terms with these features. Certainly achieving relief by such separation can rarely be dissociated from an associated feeling of guilt or depression, but whichever course promotes the least hardship, if the clients perceive relief from hardship and suffering as cowardice, principles 6 and 7 seem in conflict.

The conflict between the single client model of social work and the situational focus of much practice is further reflected in the attempt to consider principle 9 in the context of marital work, fostering work, group work and family therapy. Principle 9 ends '. . . social workers have a special responsibility to ensure the fullest possible realisation of his [the client's] rights and satisfaction of his needs.' In these cited situations it is very difficult to decide *who* is the client who has these rights. But even when it is clear who the client is, as with an infant in care where the mother has sometimes shown an inability to offer proper care, there are strong feelings among many in the social work profession that the planning for the child cannot disregard the rights of the mother. Indeed the move in juvenile courts towards separate legal representation of parents and their children in care proceedings, and even the notion of 'independent social workers' and 'guardians ad-litem' (who will also be social work professionals), indicates that the law requires not 'the fullest realisation of the client's rights and satisfaction of his needs' but a very complex balancing act which tries to minimise the negative impact on the emotional life of a child of the compromise between the duty of society to protect the child, the legal right of parents to complete responsibility for their child, and the rights of the child (which include his right to prefer to stay in a situation of pain, hardship and risk).

Many social workers are required, or choose, to identify 'situations' as the object of their attentions. The move could be popularly illustrated by the transition from the words 'child guidance' to 'family therapy' in working with childhood disturbances. The 'problems' are now commonly seen as the faulty interactions between individuals and those with whom they live or spend much of their lives. The focus is upon gaining understanding of the interactions and the part each person plays in it. Different agencies or schools of social work method place different degrees of emphasis on the responsibility for the faulty interactions. There are those who see the single individual as 'victim' of his environment or family and those who emphasise his perceptions of the world which confront him as being the important determinants of how he is to learn to react to it. Whatever approach is adopted, if the object of attention is a social situation, then the Code's goal of the realisation of one person's right and the satisfaction of his needs may be an unreasonable expectation and unrealistic goal. Work with situations is assisting people in facing the inevitable compromises which commitments to relationships press upon fulfilling unfettered rights and unrestricted needs.

Group work is one of the techniques used to communicate the personal discipline required in establishing such compromises. The essence of membership of a group with a social work purpose is the preparedness of members to accept that their personal rights and needs must be subservient to some core principles of commitment, be it only minimally to attendance at a certain place and time. The social worker will find little help from the Code in work with a group. Confidentiality is no longer something between worker and client and even more meaningless is the phrase in Principles of Practice 11, 'He respects the privacy of clients'. The whole exercise of therapeutic social work involves a sacrifice of privacy, a necessary one for the process of work to be carried out but requiring from the client a voluntary suspension of his rights to privacy. This sacrifice may be acceptable since there are expectations of personal gain from the therapeutic process. The sacrifice of privacy may however be less acceptable when it is required of people such as foster parents who do not seek personal therapeutic gain from their interaction with social workers. They may also be pressed to a deeper sacrifice of their privacy than they had bargained for, and may challenge the ethics of this. This reluctance to share with the social worker may however be used as a ground for not approving them as foster-parents but the social work model imposes a further bind upon the social worker to whom foster-parents take their problem of personal stress – should this revelation of personal weakness be ignored when the suitability of the foster-parent is reviewed?

There are other fundamental problems of contemporary social work theories and practice about which the BASW Code says nothing. The relationship between the deterministic element in both psychoanalytic and sociological investigation of 'causative' factors and the outcome of any treatment method may be profoundly influenced by the attitude the social worker adopts in relation to the historical data. It is both a moral and a therapeutic issue whether the social worker has a duty to represent a 'hopeful' or optimistic attitude whatever the data would lead him to believe. Malcolm Payne, in chapter 5 of this volume, illustrates the problem of independent professional attitudes being embroiled in agency goals of 'success' in the probation service, and the 1982 Criminal Justice Act further ties social work into a formal role within penal policy. Social work for the courts requires recommendations about disposal of cases related to factors such as the 'seriousness of the offence' and not the needs of the offender. Gone are the days of the Police Court Missionary where there was an indisputably moral position to be taken: 'I believe I can offer this offender some help.'

The future of a professional agency (in terms of its numerical size) may now be determined by whether or not it is more successful than imprisonment in reducing further offences. What then should the worker do when he sees no cause for optimism about decreasing further offending but *knows* that the potential client needs help? A code should help face this issue; perhaps agencies should only be judged on their performance with cases where they have recommended their practice as a technique of penal policy and not for moral reasons related to need. It is surprising how pervasive the acceptance has been of using 'success' rates as criteria for criticising forms of practice when no claim may ever have been made that the agency expected to 'succeed' with many of its clients. The prison service and the old Approved School system, detention centres, Community Service Orders have all been systems for disposing of certain offenders. They were imposed as punishments in many cases for the deterrent effect they would have on other people or to satisfy the needs of other people, and yet their 'reformative' success rate has been widely accepted as being of some significance. The appropriate criteria for judging them might only be the extent to which the recipient of the disposal, the client, 'feels punished' or the community identifies the person as 'having been punished'. Social work must be purposive and must only accept judgments about itself in relation to those purposes; a code should help establish this principle.

Part Two

Let me return to my central theme: How do social workers know what they ought to do? I may feel certain that I *ought* to look after my mother who has become infirm. Can I tell you, another social worker, that you ought to look after your mother who is similarly infirm? If so, from where does my authority derive? If not, then are there no values or standards from my private life which I have a right to expect colleagues or clients to share? (See Wallace and Walker, 1970.)

The relationship between personal and professional ethics is probably more complex for social workers than for members of any other profession. Less protected by office formality and restricted access than doctors, accountants and lawyers, the social worker builds expertise upon relationships with other people and this thrusts personal involvement into the middle of the arena of professional interaction. Involvement is so close between the personal and the professional value systems that there are some who argue or assume that what is appropriate in the personal world is appropriate in the professional world, and frown upon any separation or differentation between them. For example, Paul Halmos asserts that 'the sole moral justification of personalistic intervention is to enable individuals to enter into and partake in warm, empathic and genuine relationships with other persons' (1978, p. 151). Note the insertion of the presumption that a kind of intervention should be justified by 'moral' criteria rather than some criterion of pragmatic effectiveness in helping clients resolve their difficulty. A further inference is made about 'genuine' relationships which begs many questions about whether any relationship which only arises because of the worker's employment can honestly be described as 'genuine'. Must it be the test of 'genuineness' that the relationship exists for its own sake and is not 'purposive' as outlined in the definition of the professional relationship? (See Wilkes, 1981.)

When an assertion is made about what 'ought' to be done it may be a mixture of moral judgment, emotional, political and other views of the world. Consider the assertion that 'the interests of an infant *ought* to take precedence over the needs of his mother for personal fulfilment'. From where does the authority, if any, for such a statement derive? If only from themselves, or an authority only they recognise, we may ask whether it is a reasonable expectation of social workers that society will reflect, or be prepared to give financial support to, the way they view the world? Do they face the fact that *they* may be an informed, articulate minority asserting values which may not have the majority of the electorate's support?

If there is no differentiation between personal values and those of social work there are dangers of a presumptuousness which is more than paternalism. Values may have changed but the difficulty has not disappeared since Felix Biestek first bound casework principles inextricably with traditional Catholic theology, presuming belief in God, the inappropriateness of having babies without being married, and so on (Biestek, 1961). There is however a difficulty which approaches from the other direction when social work overreacts against such theological imperialism. Deriving in part from the psychoanalytic approach, views which were significantly different from some norm were treated as deviant views to be interpreted as expressions of some neurotic or pathological component in the person's psyche. Social workers become very nervous when confronted with people whose dedication and commitment to self-sacrifice exceeds the social workers' notion of 'reasonable' morality. They are inclined to seek for a pathology when assessing foster-parents who wish to care for a severely handicapped child. They may be correct to be alert but they must incorporate the humility to recognise that there are many people in the community whose values differ from theirs and may be associated with a higher vision of man's and woman's possibilities than those held by the individual social worker, or by the general class of people called social workers.

If the personal and the professional value systems are to be disentangled it will require clearer use of language in describing professional activity. Words from the personal sphere are borrowed and endowed with different shades of meaning. 'Befriending' is used of a professional task, for example in the probation service, or by Samaritans when the full, mutual, unreserved commitment of personal friendship is not intended and would not be acceptable to either client or worker. So the probation officer may offer his surname but call the client by his first name, and the Samaritan may, in his befriending, offer his first name but not part with his surname or address. Would we, in our private lives, see such unequal relationships as friendship? When Halmos invokes 'genu-ine' relationship as part of the mystery of the professional relationship, there is an aura of significance about the word, but no more than that if it does not carry the full equality or mutuality which it would in a personal relationship. In any case, even if it were a good social work model of practice, under what contractual circumstances is it right for a social worker to ask a client to open himself unreservedly?

In the next part of my discussion, I will begin to chart the territory of social workers' value judgments so that it can be ascertained which touchstones are appropriate for the refinement, analysis, and criticism of those judgments. The approach adopted to analyse this issue is to show that judgments can be categorised, for example, as 'personal values' and 'professional values'. Although some of the judgments fit into several categories, many of them can be placed in only one and for these it will be plain that they will be subject to different sets of rules from the contents of other categories.

Let us take as an example Mr Anthony, a married man, a social worker and a Roman Catholic. As a private person he believes that obedience to authority is a 'good thing' and gives it preference above other 'good things' such as personal freedom. However, in his work as a social worker he believes that the pursuit of personal autonomy is a valuable activity. It is not good in a moral way, like the assumption that it is good to love one's children, it is good because it helps the social work process have more permanent impact; it is good because he thinks it can be proved by research to be more effective than to demand obedience to the instructions of the social worker. Mr Anthony in his private life is an ardent advocate of his religion and accepts the obligation to convert other citizens to this belief which brings him so much joy. He also accepts the *ex cathedra* injunctions of his church and so believes it is wrong to use contraceptives. However, what does he do when the client in his family is getting into repeated difficulties because of the constant and repeated problems of child-rearing? A non-Catholic social worker may believe that the adoption of a simple form of contraception is an essential step in enabling the client to take greater control over his circumstances and to become more autonomous and responsible. Can Mr Anthony, therefore, be simultaneously a good man and a good social worker and a good Catholic? The recognition of the discrepancies between these 'selves' is important for each of us, if we are to come to terms with the conflicts and compromises required.

The BASW Code in its Foreword states that 'Membership of any profession entails certain obligations *beyond* those of the ordinary citizen'. It is also true, however, that the professional relationship may limit obligations. So Mr Anthony may believe it his duty to convert other citizens to his belief, but his professional duty may be to promote the religious observance of the child-in-care's own family religion, which may be Muslim.

What is the ethical position of a social worker whose understanding or analysis of the client position is founded upon a commitment to a set of personal beliefs which are not shared with his clients? Is the obligation, as writers such as Ruth Wilkes (1981) presume, to share the social worker's beliefs, or exploratory journey, 'as if' the client was a friend or fellow citizen, or must workers distance themselves and avoid imposing or proselytising to their beliefs? Can the obligation to share the existential journey towards belief be part of the professional role when there can be no expectation that training has led to workers adopting any generally shared set of beliefs? Nor has it prepared them for the position of being confronted with clients with firm sets of beliefs which impose ethical expectations which exceed the personal goals of the social worker, and may even be dismissed as reflections of a personal pathology. How does a social worker react to the New Testament injunction to forsake father and mother, sister and brother to follow Christ?

I will attempt to disentangle the many threads which interweave in situations such as that of Mr Anthony; starting with the categories 'personal values', 'professional values' and 'employers values', there are some principles of his which are clearly to be placed in one and not another. Some examples are shown in Figure 3.1 as the categories might apply to Mr Anthony.

Personal values	Professional values	Employer's values
obedience; Roman Catholicism; convert non-believers; conformity; authoritarian; anti-abortion; anti-birth control.	non-directive attitude to clients; personal autonomy for clients and encourage self-determination; Non-judgmental.	encourage conformity to social norms; assist with birth control techniques; avoid imposing worker's views on clients.

Figure 3.1

There will be some commitments that will be a member of each of these categories, such as 'conveying to the client a sense of being cared about'. A value such as this is advocated for different reasons by the 'person' of the social worker, by the 'professional' and by the employer. Mr Anthony will say that he should care about his client because his religion advocates that he should care about every other human. This may or may not override his personal attraction to, or revulsion against, a particular client who is, say, an unashamed paederast. His professional advisers will say that it greatly assists the effective outcome of the work if the client feels cared about, that is, the worker is required to give an effective impression of caring regardless of what he actually feels. His employer, perhaps a Local Authority, will say that he should give the impression of caring, not necessarily because it helps the client but because if he does not there may be public complaints which would be a politicial embarrassment. For example, responding to an aggressive, rich, articulate, elderly person who is demanding a free bus pass to which he is entitled. Thus the proof of the need for, or the justification for, such a value as caring will be entirely different if Mr Anthony is speaking with his 'personal' voice or his 'professional' voice or as an 'employee of a Local Authority'. It is vital to identify these differences; whole books have been written mistakenly presuming the coincidence between these value systems (such as Biestek, 1961).

An important benefit from identifying the source of value assertions is that when they can be shown to derive from personal belief systems and not professional sources, it cannot be presumed that they are a consensus view among social workers. It could enable a core set of common views to be identified and any additions to those views clearly assigned to those who share the same belief set. Assertions of values or principles of practice which reach beyond the consensus should then be preceded by their source; 'Catholic social workers will agree' or 'Feminists will take the view' or 'If we believe that casework should not be aimed at producing results then . . . we must persuade someone to pay social workers to pursue the moral endeavour and disregard results.' It is also a worthwhile exercise to consider some of the demands of the representatives of clients' rights as set out in the BASW discussion paper arguing that *Clients are Fellow Citizens* (BASW, 1980), to see how they fit in these sets, and to consider the conflicts posed for professional values.

The first breakdown of values into categories suggested above is into three as in Figure 3.2.

The figure illustrates the overlap between the sets of beliefs, the central shaded area indicates those values common to all three sets of values. Personal values of different social workers may include 'openness in relationships', 'obedience', 'conformity', expressed in stances which manifest radicalism, marxism, feminism, authori-

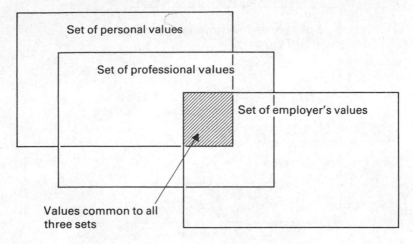

Figure 3.2

tarian attitudes, male chauvinism, conservatism, scepticism, agnos-
ticism, Christianity, Judaism, Islam, Buddhism, commitment to
others, self-protective detachment from others, etc. etc. Professional
values may include 'detachment', 'controlled emotional involvement', 'self-determination', 'individualism', 'non-critical acceptance', 'confidentiality', 'personal manipulation', and 'behaviouristic
techniques'. Employer's values may include statutory constraints
on personal liberty, formal supervisory responsibility, protection of
other citizens, offering caring relationships, detachment, provision
of services, in-depth assessment, sharing of information with other
agencies, task centred casework, abandonment of high risk cases,
adjusting clients to decisions made in the interests of others, etc.,
etc. These lists indicate the potential overlap but also the
exclusiveness of the members of different sets.

A set which has some overlap with the professional set in relation
to clients, but is not coincident with them, is the set of relations
with 'secondary' clients such as relatives of the primary client.
Secondary clients have rights which are subservient to the therapeutic needs of the primary client, and the worker's relationship
with them will therefore be different. An exploration of some
ethical problems will focus on some of the available 'sets' illustrated
by Figure 3.3.

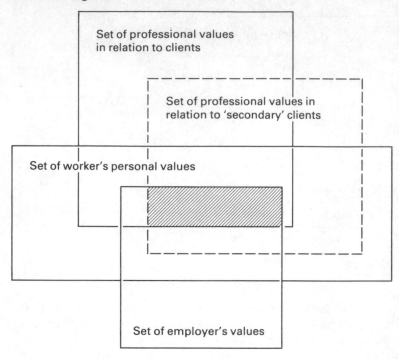

Figure 3.3

The importance of thinking clearly about the difference in relationship between social workers and clients and social workers and 'secondary' persons can be illustrated by the anger and confusion of some foster-parents in their relationship with social workers. The tools and language of social workers, as well as their record systems, are dominated by the model of worker and client, of health and pathology. The foster-parents, particularly during the assessment stage, will experience themselves as seen through the magnifying glass designed to search out pathological conditions, but both social worker and foster-parent will become entrapped by this technique. Even the invitation from the social worker to the applicants to 'tell me about any difficulties you are having in your marriage' places a double bind upon both parties because it is an invitation to a therapeutic relationship but the material shared by the foster-parents cannot be removed from consideration when the judgment is being made with regard to their suitability as foster-parents. Social workers have not found a satisfactory word to describe those people with whom they have useful working relationships, who are not social workers and in relation to whom the social workers exercise a 'helping' or 'enabling', 'influential' relationship but where the contract is not towards a 'therapeutic' goal.

The important message to be derived from this analytical model is that there will be values in each of the sets which are not in other sets and which may be in direct conflict with some of the values in other sets. For example an employer's view may reflect the law in relation to child care and thus within his set might be the value 'unless parents have requested care, or obvious neglect can be established in a court, a child should be brought up within his natural family' (see Section 2, 1980 Child Care Act and Section 1, 1969 Children and Young Person's Act). This value would also fall within the set for 'secondary clients', if the family was a strict Muslim one. However, the social worker may have strong personal values which reflect a liberated, feminist, framework which would exclude from it many of the values within the Muslim parents' set if the client were a teenage girl. Similarly, the professional values which might be reflected in practice with the teenage Muslim girl, whilst containing 'emotional acceptance' cannot contain acceptance of rebellious views without excluding itself from the set of employer's values and from the set held by 'secondary clients'. These value sets may be modified by the severity of conflict as expressed – the employer's position on this case will alter if the father seriously beats his child to enforce conformity and the court makes a care order. The obligation to try to meet the total needs of the child in care will then push the 'set' of employer's values into greater coincidence with the set of professional values and some greater overlap between the worker's personal values and the client's value system. This very move, however, places greater strains on the worker not to impose 'personal values' on the 'professional' values by trading on the client's rebellious feelings to 'recruit' her to values which may only store up more serious future conflict problems for her in society. This may be more obvious in situations where children in care in residential homes become involved in unionised battles with the employing authority and the children may model their future relationship with authority upon this experience.

In order to think clearly about the influence of belief systems it is necessary to point out the error of the very tempting assumption that morally good personal conduct is to be expected to give rise to professionally therapeutic effects. Even if a utilitarian defines good conduct as that which produces the best effects in general, it cannot be assured to do so for every individual. But those whose morality surpasses utilitarianism may infer that 'love' which is expressed in religious or philosophical terms is inseparable from that relationship which will be expected to have good practical outcomes from clients or patients. Fr Biestek's seven principles (1961) are the classic example of Catholic theology and mysticism used to amplify the three principles which may be clinically justifiable into seven. Good conduct may or may not lead to therapeutic effects. As Iris Murdoch's essay *The Sovereignty of Good* (1970) concludes, 'Love is the general name of the quality of attachment and it is capable of infinite degradation . . . but is . . . the force that joins us to the world through Good,' and, further, 'The humble man . . . sees the *pointlessness* of virtue and its unique value and endless extent of its demand.'

At a more superficial level are the problems posed for social workers by the preference for the application of a personal style over client needs. For example, the rejection by some social workers of methods which they find uncongenial, when there are no other alternatives available. They may oppose electro-convulsive therapy for the profoundly depressed or may reject the notion of punishment for offenders even when 'counselling' proves ineffective. Again, they might resist undertaking inspection of the premises of 'caring' persons, be they foster-parents or natural parents with histories of child neglect. The Malcolm Page Inquiry Report (Essex County Council, 1981) illustrates this problem.

A further source of confusion about the professional value set is its close association with only one model of client contact – the voluntary relationship where the client brings his own anxiety about his problems and the object of the exercise is to assist the client to come to better terms with his own internal or social situation. This is a relationship with many degrees of freedom which are often not present in the most common reality of clients' lives, and particularly in the major employing agencies in this country: social services departments or the probation service. If the goal is to influence the client and not necessarily to relieve his anxiety, then the repertoire of professional techniques may include real or implied threats, criticism of values or conduct, and the show of anger. Many of these are not included in social workers' sets of personal values although they may be included in the repertoire of personal conduct. I may, for example, believe that social behaviour should be subject to rational discussion, though I do lose my temper with my children, sometimes irrationally and in a bullying manner. Such behaviour would be subject to much more severe criticism if it occurred in my professional practice than it would within the home. If social workers went about expressing their feelings to the clients it would be regarded as a very unsatisfactory form of professional conduct. It is, however, well within the repertoire of social workers to influence people by a conscious use of a display of anger or indignation, this emotion being simulated for its possible effect.

There are other techniques considered appropriate to the client situation which would be regarded as anathema within one's friendships, for example, deliberate manipulation. In casework it may be rationalised as being enabling to the other within the context of some bond of trust. In some forms of groupwork, however, the leader's or consultant's role is entirely manipulative and in such circumstances Paul Halmos's resort to 'genuineness' in relation (1978) can only be sustained within a much wider context of established trustworthiness. However, the position of a member of a group who perceives himself being asked to 'perform' the role of being a member of a group and to discuss a subject which no one in the group has any investment in debating, as happens in some group processes, is very ambiguous. Is such a performance a denial of the need for any 'genuineness' in relationships? It would seem so.

It has so far been suggested that the association of professional value sets for relationships and personal value sets is a misleading guide to good professional practice. There are many other good reasons for keeping them separate. As private people we choose to whom we relate. We can stand in a crowded lift as if we were alone: among those to whom we relate we can pursue relationships which are encouraging and accepting, or rejecting. As social workers we are rarely so free. We must relate in order to work. We might make later adjustments if the matching is detrimental but we have to relate well enough to get something started. To relate as the social worker inclines is therefore unprofessional; the model of private conduct is not compatible with professional conduct and therefore cannot be used as an appropriate model without many reservations.

The moral implications of some necessary forms of social work practice need a closer examination than they have had. Consider the social worker responsible for a young person who has had many years in council care in homes. In order to carry out his statutory duties he must attempt to induce the child to talk about himself and his thoughts, feelings, wishes and dreams. A person will only share these intimacies with someone with whom he has a relationship, unless the recounting has been transformed into a performance art such as poetry or literary expression. The social worker is therefore obliged to try to draw the child into a relationship for no other purpose than to satisfy the social worker's job requirements. It is exceptional if the worker offers important parts of himself or herself to the child's personal social world. The relationship is part of a statutory and financial transaction from which only the social worker benefits financially. He is at a loss if the young person fails to participate in some kind of relationship. The fieldworker is expected to seduce the young person or child emotionally into a relationship which only the worker may need. In practice the social worker is one of a chain 'relating' to the young person over the years, at a rate of one every two years, or less. The child who has fallen in with this strategy has received more than adequate experience in developing promiscuous relationships, relationships with ulterior purposes and which have no inherent personal significance. When he or she grows out of the Children's Home environment and drifts out into the grey world of young people with no family ties and sits in the main line station, or West End café, seeking a pick-up relationship of some kind which will offer a bed, or money, he or she has been well trained for this promiscuity. If his or her activity of forming superficial relationships for money is described as prostitution how is it essentially different from the social worker's activity in relation to the young person in care? Is it better or worse to receive payment for transactions involving one's body than for transactions involving emotions and the inner person, or soul? It may be perceived as an overstatement to use the word 'prostitution' in relation to social work activity, but we must recognise the hypocrisy inherent in denying the difference between the personal and professional worlds. If the hypocrisy is not denied but is accepted as an essential tool then it loses its shame and a myth and source of irrational guilt is removed. This is a difficult hurdle to leap. Hypocrisy can carry with it the definition 'the simulation of goodness' with some positive connotations; the hypocrite may be a pretender or dissembler but the motivation for this may be entirely proper. If I am very angry or depressed because of a client's failure to meet the goals which he had set for himself then I will weigh very carefully the extent to which it will help him if I openly share my 'genuine' feelings; most likely I will dissemble or pretend the 'therapeutically prescribed' set of responses to the client in the hope that there will be a positive and optimistic echo of feedback.

The professional social worker views a hard world; the task is made harder because of the conscious or unconscious attempts to deny its hardness and cynical aspects. He is required to manipulate people and their relationships, and must learn the art of appearing to care when his natural feeling is not to care. To survive as a private person and to do his work well he must sometimes operate within a mode of 'bad faith', a lack of absolute honesty in the relationship (Sartre, 1957). To fulfil expectations which are necessary for the good response of the client, he must put on an act because to be himself may well be self-indulgent and destructive. For example, much professional and political literature calls for social workers to implement programmes called 'community care' but an honest appraisal may well find that neither the community nor the employers (in the form of local councillors) actually do feel caring about the clients and in many situations are overtly hostile to social work objectives. He may devote himself to real personal caring in his relationships with some clients, and that may well be what they desperately need, but there is a strangeness both about being paid to form relationships and about pretending that the social worker represents the community. A salesman has no illusions, his relationships have an end in view – selling the goods. A social worker may sometimes be able to see the relationship in such simply purposive terms but sometimes the client need appears to be for a relationship for itself: a curious phenomenon to be paid for. The self-protection which a prostitute adopts as a professional stand is that she acts out the role to meet the physical bodily needs of her clients and allows them to act out their fantasies, but it is when an element of real relationship enters into the transaction that she will become uneasy at the breakdown of the professional boundary. Where is the self-protection for a social worker who is paid to act out a response to the inner self of the client?

If the employers' set of expectations differ from the professional or personal ideals then what can they 'reasonably expect' from professionals as employees? What kinds of protection can they offer to social workers against the emotional hazards and stresses which the work may impose if there is no way of containing the response to the personal demands of the exposure to clients with intense emotional needs?

The requirement laid upon the professional is to conduct himself in such a way as to produce the most benefit for his client. It is not enough to *feel* good about the pattern of service provision. There is sometimes a contrast between efficient professionalism and disorganised emotional commitment; there may be a conflict between worker-centred models of practice and client-centred models. The social work profession has not always given primacy to evolving methods which are determined by the client's perception of the interaction and the fulfilment of his psychic needs in a manner he can make use of. Often the client has been expected to adapt to the professional's preferences, as is common to most other professions.

This chapter has so far been an attempt to release thinking about social work values from the confusing embrace of an idealistic universalism, the belief that all social workers at heart view the world identically, that they will agree on personal value systems and that they work in what is near enough to a Utopian world in which employers find the social worker's view of the world entirely convincing and are prepared to provide the wherewithal to promote it. There is plenty of evidence that this universalism is not useful nor appropriate nor attainable and that more constructive progress will be derived from greater precision in specifying what is inherent to professional social work as it can be practised.

If social work thinking is to move beyond an amalgam of personal assertions of what 'ought' to be done, it must move into statements which can be discussed and examined or even tested. These must be of the form 'if A is the required objective then B is the principle or method which should be adopted'. In statements of ethics then the objective A in such a statement may be a set of beliefs about the nature of the world and man's proper place in it, and B will be a means of expressing it in action.

Part Three

In accord with the criticisms set out so far of the BASW Code and the more stringent models for statements which have been advocated, can the discussion of a social work ethic be moved forward?

The purists' dedication to the single client focus and the much-abused absolute principles such as 'confidentiality' would seem to require a reconciliation which can be shared with and appreciated by clients. Adopting the model of good practice set out above we might say the following.

Principle A   If a social worker is to reconcile his personal integrity with the compromises of principle which his agency requires, then he should maintain a *trustworthy* relationship with his client and this will require him to keep the client aware of the nature, duties and functions of the agency and the social worker's tasks within that agency.

This principle faces the tension between the 'helping' and 'policing' mode. Trustworthiness also requires honesty with the client about the judgments about him which the social worker is making in his head as well as in his written assessments. It can also be the bridge between individualistic personal treatment principles and those of joint work with couples, families and groups and also task-oriented work such as conciliation work with divorcing couples. It also, in its honesty, allows the client to withdraw if the obligations of trustworthiness and sharing information are too much to bear. Fantasies and illusions about the worker and the agency can be confronted or dissolved (Rees, 1978). This latter aspect could be strengthened by a further principle:

Principle B   If his work is to be in contact with the real world a social worker should give respectful attention to the client's view of the world.

This is a stronger position to adopt than the implications in notions such as acceptance, which misleadingly suggests that client's lifestyle and choices are always acceptable to social workers. It can accommodate the right of clients consciously to choose criminality, and to unmake that choice, and thus avoids the presumption that to choose criminal activity is a manifestation of a wholly determining personal history. It can also contain the extreme Laingian view that all conduct, no matter how bizarre, is a communication capable of interpretation within the client's own frame of reference. Principle B should however be associated with another:

Principle C   In order to work from a firm foundation the social worker must maintain contact with and respect for the reality of the client's world and his perception of it.

The social worker can only understand the commitment of the client to his perceptions of the world if he has made the effort to check the actual circumstances of the client's experience. Without such knowledge it is very difficult to find the point where resentment about the real effects of the outside world becomes paranoia. In ethnic minority groups this may be exceptionally difficult for workers, and some clients need very skilled help to establish the boundary for themselves between real effects and imagined fears. For example, the teenage Asian girl's accounts of arranged marriage or abduction to Asia and fears of her parents' physical abuse are appealing to feminists seeking to separate a child from her male-dominated culture but the same accounts can be the manipulations of a girl interested only in maintaining her relationship with a white boyfriend. The worker's view may be that it would be best for the client to abandon his stand, for example his running battle with the world, but he will have a much greater chance of convincing his client of this if his client perceives himself in the first instance as being 'understood' in what he believes about the world, and why he views it the way he does.

An illustration of the issues to which this principle gives rise may be drawn from Christopher Dowrick's attempt to integrate marxism and psychoanalysis (Dowrick, 1983). He writes of a woman who suffers an attack of mania, is admitted to psychiatric hospital, loses her ill paid living-in hotel job, is then eased out of hospital into sheltered housing and a day centre: Miss O'Brien is now assured of decent accommodation and a supportive network to meet her emotional needs. She feels she is better off. Adherence to principle C might allow the criterion of the client's feeling better off to provide a ground for feeling that a job has been well done. But Dowrick cannot leave the matter there . . . : 'it may well be that I should have given her more encouragement to return to the hotel . . . and helped her to make links with other underpaid workers in the local hotels.' If the idea and ideals of this kind are not derived from the client's thoughts then what authority can come from the contractual relationship with the client to go beyond the duty to promote courses which enable the client to feel she is better off? The desire of the worker not to co-operate with the operation of the free commercial competition of the capitalist system may be laudable in his own private transactions but this does not seem to provide a moral basis for putting the client, and possibly the hotel's economy, at risk.

The extent of exploring carefully the respect for the client's view of the world could perhaps more definitely be delineated by a further principle.

Principle D   If he is to avoid unjustifiable domination of his clients the worker's personal feelings should be subjugated to the demand to respond to the client's problem in the most beneficial manner.

This is very far-reaching if it puts to the test of client benefit all the social worker's preferences for working practices and models of management. It may raise questions about whether 'consensus' or 'democratic' management styles are the best way to deliver the goods of client services or whether they might prove more time-wasting and less effective than more charismatic or authoritarian leadership styles.

On the other wing the last two principles C and D provide ground for examining aspects of psychoanalytic models. There has been little attention directed at the lack of rspect for the integrity of the client which is reflected in the presumption that a client's action (or even worse his statements) are to be seen *only* as *expressions* of inner states and not as having a parallel validity as actions or factual statements. So the social worker's record may read: 'Jones seen at office, very angry and responding immaturely to attempts to help him see how manipulative his behaviour was . . .', but such a record does not include the fact that Jones had waited an hour in the waiting room before seeing the social worker and that he was very concerned that he might not get the necessary letter to the DHSS office in time before it closed. The dangers of political 'reinterpretation' of the client's social world are not considered in the BASW Code as it stands. These principles C and D can provide an acknowledgment that 'reinterpretation' can be applied because of psychic bias in the worker as well as political bias and emphasise the acceptance in a democracy that reality has many facets to it and provokes many responses.

The BASW Code Principles of Practice 10.1 calls upon social workers to contribute to the formulation and implementation of policies for human welfare with only the constraint that they should not be inhuman policies. This gives no assistance in resolving the problems of oversimplified models of causation and straightforward deterministic philosophies. Social workers may provide the information upon which paternalistic policies or social engineering can be implemented. The moral issue is crystallised in the question, 'What ought the social worker to do when faced with a predicted 'failure' in client assessment?' There must remain a means of escape for clients from arbitrary policies and a philosophical space to allow therapeutic hope to enter the interaction.

Social work, whilst acknowledging the value of systematic attempts to understand human behaviour, must assert a philosophy which can contain the belief that the determining frameworks, psychological or social, are susceptible to the transcendence of the spirit. Some of the misgivings arise from misunderstandings of the nature of the social sciences by associating them with the models of the physical sciences of the nineteenth century: the popularised model which says of physical circumstances 'If *that* in the past then *this* in the future'. For example, the view that maternal deprivation as a child will produce delinquent conduct. This model is better replaced by one which says 'If *that* in the past then the probability of *this* in the future is P'. Furthermore the relationship between the single individual and the large sample upon which the prediction is valid is affected by some principles of uncertainty. The general principle may be true but it is not true with certainty for any one individual, unless it is a statement of the past rather than the future. An unpredictable external event such as the amputation of a leg could take one individual right out of the sample for whom the prediction was valid, if they were physically normal persons.

In ethical terms the challenge to determinism must somehow be asserted by social workers; an attempt to express this could be the following principle.

Principle E   A social worker, whilst valuing the contribution of the social sciences to the establishing of general understandings about human conduct, must respect the uncertain nature of knowledge in human affairs.

This uncertainty arises not only from the inherently probabilistic, rather than directly causal, connections between facts or circumstances and subsequent events or conduct but also from the influence of time on those connections. The person confronting the social worker is not the same person this year that he was last year and will not be the same person when he leaves the interview that he was when he entered the room. The increment of change may be minute but it may be profound and it is essential to the theory of social work and to the ethics of its implementation that this be recognised.

There is growing appreciation that the philosophies or paradigms of the pure sciences have undergone a revolution since the nineteenth century and that they no longer have the straightforward philosophies of cause and effect, of material facts, or even of time which popular models associate with them. The impact of some of their new philosophies on the models used by social scientists may in due course provide routes for the interaction of social work with social circumstances to be incorporated. In the meantime, however, whilst the simplistic models are still being propagated, social work will have to assert the principle of uncertainty which at core derives from every man's right to confront the inevitable and to reject it (see de Vries, 1981; Capra, 1976).

4 Responsibility in social work

Gavin Fairbairn

Introduction

The Code of Ethics for Social Work begins with the statement that 'Social work is a professional activity. Implicit in its practice are ethical principles which prescribe the professional responsibility of the social worker' (Objectives, para. 1). I think this is a mistaken view; it has I think got 'the cart before the horse': any set of ethical principles for social work must begin with a consideration of the responsibilities the social worker has. In this paper I will discuss these responsibilities and the responsibilities of social work agencies, in the light of the Code's frequent reference to them. I will also examine the responsibility of the social work client especially as this relates to the responsibilities of social workers.

Some different senses of 'responsibility'

The terms 'responsible' and 'responsibility' can each be used in a number of different ways and before looking specifically at responsibility in social work, I wish to consider some of these uses (see also Hart, 1965; Downie, 1971; Benn and Peters, 1959).

(a) The attribution of responsibility is sometimes used to indicate that a person has caused a state of affairs; in this sense a person who is instrumental in bringing about an event or state of affairs is 'causally responsible' for it.[1] Causal responsibility may be grounds for moral blame (or credit where a desirable state of affairs is brought about). However, this is not always the case. Consider, for example, a driver who hits a pedestrian when driving his car. He is causally responsible for the person's injuries because his hitting the man brought them about. In addition he may or may not be morally blameworthy. If he causes the person's injuries and subsequent death because he deliberately drives at him or because he is driving recklessly, then his being causally responsible makes him morally culpable. The moral element arises because of the intention of the driver or because of his negligence. On the other hand he cannot be morally blamed if he was driving safely and the pedestrian stepped out without warning.

It is difficult to determine the extent to which social workers are causally responsible for events or situations which come about in the course of their practice because there are so many diverse causes acting upon clients. For example, although a social worker who decides to withdraw day care facilities from an elderly person who has refused to use them regularly may be considered partially causally responsible if the elderly person has an accident, we would not say that she was solely causally responsible for it. Again, although a social worker is clearly causally responsible for the separation of a mother and child when she takes the child into care, she is not solely responsible for the child's psychological state after removal from the mother, even though her action is included in the causal network leading to it.

(b) Second, 'responsibility' may be used to mean the same as 'duty'; it makes no difference whether we say that a person is responsible for doing something or that he has a duty to do it. For example, a care assistant whose duty is to care for the elderly in a residential home is responsible for doing so.

The Code sometimes uses 'obligation' and 'commitments' in contexts where 'responsibility' and 'responsibilities' or 'duty' and 'duties' could be substituted with little if any change of meaning. For example, when it is asserted that 'Members of a profession have obligations to their clients, to their employers' (Foreword, para. 3), the terms 'responsibilities' or 'duties' could equally well have been used. And in relation to the statement that social workers have a 'responsibility to help individuals, families, groups and communities' (Statement of Principles, para. 7), it is asserted that 'The social worker has a commitment to serve these purposes with integrity and skill' (Statement of Principles, para. 8), All of these terms seem to me to be used to mean the same in the Code. In general what is being referred to when the Code uses such terms is what a social worker should or should not do in virtue of his role as a social worker. Although in this chapter I am talking about responsibility in social work, my comments may therefore also be of relevance in situations where the discussion of what we in social work ought to do takes place in terms of duty, obligation or commitment.

(c)   A third sense of 'responsibility' is a matter of 'accountability' and is closely related to duty, in that a person who has a duty is accountable for its performance. A person who is accountable is liable to have to explain or justify what he has done, or has not done. A person is usually accountable for something in particular or in a particular context and accountability is always attached to a particular role. For example, it is in virtue of his role as an airline pilot that a man who flies planes for British Airways is accountable for the safety of his passengers. And it is in virtue of her role that a social worker is accountable for the way in which she performs her professional duties and to some extent for the results of her professional activity. Accountability may lead to blame or praise and may or may not be morally relevant depending on the particular context. Consider, for example, a lifeguard whose duty it is to save, or attempt to save, the lives of swimmers in difficulty. Because of this role he is accountable for the lives of swimmers who drown. If a person drowns because the lifeguard was drunk on duty, or asleep, instead of patrolling the beach, his accountability means that he can be morally blamed. On the other hand, if he fails to save a swimmer because of sudden leg cramp whilst attempting to reach her, he will be accountable, but his account of his attempt to fulfil his duty will leave him free of blame even though someone has died.

(d)   The final sense of 'responsibility' I wish to consider is that in which people are said to be 'responsible' when what is meant is that they are trustworthy. A person who is said to be responsible in this way will often have a serious attitude towards the world and his effects on it, and will take his duties seriously. In this way, for example, a trustworthy employee may be thought of as 'responsible' enough to be given important and 'responsible tasks'. Someone who is treated as a responsible person is relied upon to perform duties to the best of his ability and to make justifiable decisions about courses of action. This sense of 'responsibility' in which persons are said to be responsible or not is often used to convey some kind of moral approval, as for example, when a person is said to have acted responsibly in an emergency situation. The attribution of responsibility in this sense depends to some extent upon the intellectual level and/or mental state of the individual in question. Very young children, the profoundly mentally handicapped and the severely mentally ill are normally treated as if they are not, and are not capable of being, responsible in the sense of trustworthy, and therefore as if they are incapable of taking decisions for themselves, or of being relied upon by others.

I have outlined some different senses of responsibility and some of the ways in which the terms 'responsible' and 'responsibility' may be used. These different senses and uses will often overlap with and sometimes conflict with one another. Some examples might help to make this clear. A person who is causally responsible for something may be deemed either 'responsible' or 'irresponsible' in my fourth sense. He will be deemed 'responsible' in cases where his causal responsibility relates to his having been deliberately instrumental in bringing about some desirable result, for example by acting wisely in an emergency situation. He will be deemed 'irresponsible' in cases where his causal responsibility relates to an undesirable outcome, for example if has caused an accident by reckless and unattentive driving. Instances also occur where all four senses of responsibility are involved. Consider, for example, a person who has a duty (or responsibility) to perform certain functions, who is accountable in a certain role and who therefore has to account for (i.e. explain and justify) his actions and omissions to act, and results which follow from them. In cases where his decisions and actions mean he is causally responsible for desirable outcomes he may be said to be 'responsible' in my fourth sense and where they have had undesirable consequences he may be said to be 'irresponsible' in this sense. In these cases the person's duty and accountability, and his having been causally responsible for the occurrence of an event (i.e. instrumental in bringing it about), mean that he is then judged by the basically moral criteria of the fourth sense of responsibility I have discussed.

The possibility that a person accountable in a particular role, for the performance of certain duties, may have been 'responsible' (in my fourth sense) in making a decision or in an action, even though a bad consequence has followed, is often ignored. The difficulty here is in determining how we might decide that a person has, in this sense, acted 'responsibly' in a given instance without reference to the actual outcome (which may be influenced by factors unknown at the time the decision to act in this way was made). It is perhaps because of this difficulty that stress in, for example, social work, tends to be put upon an individual's accountability to the agency for carrying out given procedures (acting 'by the book'), rather than upon their responsibility as individual people. Later in this chapter I will discuss some of the difficulties which arise because of the tendency to view social workers' responsibility in terms of accountability where causal responsibility for occurrences is taken to imply 'irresponsibility' and hence moral blame, on the part of individuals or whole agencies. I will suggest that greater stress should be laid upon 'personal responsibility' in social work.

In the next section I will try to make clear which sense of responsibility is being referred to in each case. Thereafter I hope that the context of my comments will help to make it clear which sense is intended at each point.

The responsibility of the social worker

The Code states generally that 'Members of a profession have obligations to their clients, to their employers, to each other, to colleagues in other disciplines and to society' (Foreword, para. 3). 'Obligation' here means responsibility in sense (b), that is, as duty. Social workers have very wide-ranging responsibilities to a number of different groups. They are responsible to (that is, they have duties towards) clients, to the agency by which they are employed, to the community which funds their agency, and to society in general. Since they have these responsibilities in virtue of their role as social workers rather than as citizens, they are accountable to these groups for the performance of these duties. In addition they are accountable to their profession and, in the case of social workers who are members of a professional association such as BASW, to that association. The individual social worker may also be said to be accountable to herself in that her integrity as a person depends upon her acting in ways that she would expect of herself, that are congruent with her personal value system; in a sense the social worker, to maintain her personal integrity, has to account inwardly for what she does in practice.

The relative importance that the social worker places on these different responsibilities will be influenced by her conception of the social work task and the model of social work that she embraces, and this will influence the methods and approaches she adopts in her work. For example, a social worker who sees the task in terms of assisting clients in their 'personal growth' will construe her responsibilities (that is, the duties for the performance of which she must account), differently than another who sees it largely in terms of assisting clients with practical problems such as managing finances and developing strategies for child care.

To some extent the way the social worker construes her responsibilities and the relative importance she places upon them will depend upon the particular client group with whom she is involved and the agency function she performs. A social worker specialising in cases involving alleged child abuse may consider her responsibility largely as accountability for carrying out (and the duty to carry out) required procedures. One working in intermediate treatment, on the other hand, may emphasise the responsibility (or duty) to provide a suitable role model and facilitate self-esteem and moral awareness in young people. And social workers involved with the physically disabled or elderly may see the responsibilities or duties of the task largely in terms of obtaining and distributing benefits such as domiciliary services, adequate and appropriate housing and DHSS benefits such as attendance and mobility allowances, while those working with the mentally ill may emphasise the responsibility (or duty) to facilitate clients' ability to cope with their psychological problems while living in the community. The nature of the agency in which the social worker is employed will also affect her view of her responsibilities. For example, statutory and voluntary agencies have different aims and different commitments in terms of the services they provide and the function they fulfil, and different responsibilities expressed in the Code may be emphasised as a result. The structure of the agency, for example the extent to which social workers are allowed by managers to make largely independent casework decisions, may also be important in determining the way in which they view their task and hence their responsibilities (or duties).

Accountability in social work

Social workers are accountable for all aspects of their practice, from the way in which they manage their caseload and administrative tasks to the decisions they make and the actions they take in casework or in other interventions with individuals or groups. I said earlier that a person who is accountable is liable to explain and justify his decisions and actions to others, and is liable to praise or blame according as his actions seem to be justified or not. However, accountability is very often seen simply in terms of the allocation of blame when things go wrong. In social work this negative view of accountability may be noted in situations where agencies may be construed as having been negligent in some way. Such a view is regrettable because of its negative effects on practice.

Public reaction to situations where social workers may be construed as negligent is commonly expressed in the media by blaming the agency in question for 'lack of care' or for 'being irresponsible'. A typical example of such a situation is where a child, returned to parents known to have caused it non-accidental injury in the past, dies as the result of further non-accidental injury. Again, where an elderly person, living at home, suffers harm which it is possible to link to insufficient support, irresponsibility is alleged. In the first of these cases it is interesting to note that public reaction is sometimes equally strong where children are removed from parents suspected of neglect or ill-treatment, when the grounds upon which such removal takes place are construed as inadequate by the media. In the second it is worth noting that accusations of lack of support might be made even though the old person in question had been offered and had refused domiciliary services. This is illustrative of what might be called the 'someone must do something' attitude to statutory social services agencies. Social workers will be familiar with the belief often manifested by relatives, neighbours, clients themselves and representatives of other agencies, that social workers are able and entitled, even obliged (in the sense of having a duty), to do something in relation to anyone considered to be in need or in danger.

Attending to accountability in terms of the possibility of being blamed when things go wrong can reduce the effectiveness of social work interventions because social workers who see their responsibility in this way may act in ways which are counterproductive in terms of social work's aims, as expressed, for example, in the Code. In addition it may actually increase rather than decrease the problems addressed and limit the extent to which social workers may act in accordance with what they believe is best for clients. An example might help to make these points clear.

Mr Stewart, who was diagnosed 'paranoid schizophrenic', had had two compulsory admissions to psychiatric hospitals. Although his delusions affected his 23-year-old daughter who was unemployed and lived at home, Mr Stewart held down a responsible job and outside the home there was no known evidence of disturbance. A year after his last admission Mr Stewart's daughter asked her general practitioner for help because she thought her father was 'going off again'; her request amounted to a demand that 'someone should do something'. A joint visit was arranged with the general practitioner, a consultant psychiatrist and a psychiatric social worker. Mr Stewart's condition did not meet the criteria for compulsory admission and so he was left in the community; indeed there was agreement between all three professionals that although Mr Stewart was clearly disturbed the real problem at this time was the breakdown of the relationship between Mr Stewart and his daughter. Because of this the social worker offered casework help. This offer was willingly accepted by Mr Stewart and less willingly accepted by his daughter. After some weeks Mr Stewart asked that the social worker should not call again because after each visit his daughter was unbearable (it should be noted that what the daughter meant by 'someone doing something' was that they should take her father into hospital again). Difficulties arose for the social services department when Mr Stewart's daughter appealed in turn to her local councillor, the Mayor of the Council, the local branch of the Association for Mental Health (MIND) and finally to her Member of Parliament, to intervene and 'get something done'. In response to pressure from each of these in turn, the social worker who had been involved was directed by management to investigate Mr Stewart's condition. The social worker made clear her opinion that continued approaches would result in Mr Stewart's developing a dislike for the department; however, she went as instructed. After a time Mr Stewart began to develop paranoid suspicions that the social worker was gathering information in order to try to get him 'inside' again. Whereas at the termination of their initial contract Mr Stewart had said that he would contact the social worker should he feel the need, by the end of several months of being intermittently bothered by her despite his expressed wish that she stay away, he was refusing to even open his door to her and threatening to take court action to keep her away from his property.

In this case, viewing accountability in terms of blame resulted in a bad outcome. The department's worries about being blamed in the event of anything going seriously wrong resulted in their persisting in visiting Mr Stewart when pressurised by others. As a result of this continued attention when he had explicitly said that he wished his contact with social services to cease, Mr Stewart refused to see the social worker ever again. Whereas he had been amenable to asking for and receiving help if and when he felt that he needed it, he now said that he wanted no contact with social workers under any circumstances. More seriously it was also possible that the continued bothering of Mr Stewart by the social services department actually exacerbated this condition as he gathered more and more fuel for his suspicion that people (including the social services department) were 'out to get' him.

In the case of Mr Stewart the social services department, viewing its accountability negatively, acted in a way that was counter-productive. Adopting such a view of the social worker's accountability may also result in actions being taken for the wrong reasons. For example, there may be a tendency towards making decisions that make the department look caring, efficient and right-minded rather than those that are thought to serve the best interests of individual clients. Faced with a situation in which they are likely to be blamed if things go wrong, social workers may decide against such measures as have even a moderate chance of a bad outcome. A child might be taken into care more because of the fear of bad publicity in the unlikely event of a tragedy than because of the risk to the child which constitutes the nominal reason for its being taken into care; an elderly person might be persuaded to accept a place in an elderly person's home because of pressure brought to bear by relatives who threaten that if anything happens (by which they mean injury) to their elderly relative, they will make trouble for the department; social workers might persist in offering casework service to an individual or family beyond the point where this seems strictly necessary 'just in case' something goes wrong.

In this type of case, social workers act as they do because they are afraid of the possible consequences rather than because they have decided that their action will be of positive benefit. The social worker concerned might even believe that the action she is taking is likely to be harmful to the individual concerned. In view of the limited availability of labour, power and other resources, these decisions may seem to represent irresponsible and unethical use of resources which might have been better used in relation to others whose needs are greater. Where the social worker thinks that the decision might actually be harmful to individuals, or where she has entered into self-deceit to prevent herself from thinking this, it is clear that she is performing actions which are morally wrong in terms of her own value system.

The above examples illustrate the fact that action which might seem responsible because it reduces the risk of some bad outcomes from happening might seem irresponsible from another point of view. Similar processes to these work within other 'caring disciplines'. For example, Thomas Scheff (1966, ch. 4) has claimed that there is a tendency in medicine for doctors to diagnose illness when none is present more often than fail to recognise it when it is present. Doctors, Scheff claims, are more likely to be blamed for failing to treat when necessary than they are for treating when unnecessary. Because of this they tend to overtreat rather than undertreat in a similar way to that in which social workers tend to intervene rather than refrain from intervention when there is a chance that refraining might have undesirable consequences which will come to light.

The Code asserts that 'The profession accepts a responsibility to encourage and facilitate the self-realisation of the individual person' (Statement of Principles, para. 6). It is beyond the scope of this chapter to discuss in any detail what might be meant by the expression 'self-realisation' or why it might be thought preferable to the term 'self-determination' which the Code avoids because it 'sounds a little too open-ended' (Commentary on Statement of Principles). However, it seems likely that it is concerned in some way with the growth of individual autonomy and personal responsibility. Viewing responsibility as accountability in the sense of being blameworthy seems likely to limit the extent to which social workers are willing to encourage the growth of clients in this direction. A social worker who construes her responsibility dominantly in terms of her accountability for the results of her actions may be excessively involved with guarding her *reputation* as a caring professional to the detriment of her ability or willingness to allow clients to choose their own future actions and states. It is perhaps partly because of this that social work, in common with other caring disciplines, can tend towards paternalism.

Where a bad outcome follows a social work decision or action it is not necessarily the case that those who are responsible for it are blameworthy; decisions that are made in good faith may be followed by results which are undesirable but this in itself does not mean that the decision in question was the wrong one. It may be the case, for example, that just as bad or even worse consequences might have followed from another decision. An old person might sustain accidental injuries while awaiting allocation to an elderly person's home but it is worth noting that had she been admitted, some other old person might have had to wait; and this second old person might have had a worse accident while waiting.

Surely what is important is that social workers should be able to account, not so much for the results of their decisions, as for the way in which they reached them. In order that she should be able to account for her decisions, the social worker must make them with good knowledge of the circumstances. They must in other words be made from a state of personal certainty, based on sound argument, that they constitute the best possible alternative. In situations where she is involved in making joint decisions, the social worker will be accountable for making as clear as possible her thoughts and feelings about the best course of action in order that decisions which are made are consonant with her considered professional views.

The responsibility of the client in social work

The Code asserts that the social worker 'will respect his clients as individuals and will seek to ensure that their dignity, individuality, rights and responsibility shall be safeguarded' (Principles of Practice, para. 10.2). This point is elaborated in the commentary: 'particular attention should be paid lest a person suffers loss of dignity or rights by the very act of becoming a client.' By safeguarding the dignity and individuality of clients the Code presumably means something like treating clients with respect as human beings with individual needs and aspirations. However, it is less clear what 'loss of rights' and consequently what the safeguarding of clients' rights might consist in. This question is one which is worthy of more attention than it can be given here. For example, in considering it adequately questions would have to be raised about the status of different rights and whether there are any rights which are natural or inherent rights or whether all rights are conferred or granted. Indeed the whole question of what constitutes a right and whether there are any such things as rights is in itself a complex issue which deserves attention. Although such detailed questions cannot be tackled here it should be noted that it is not clear what rights the Code is referring to; whether, for example, these are basic 'human rights', 'welfare rights' or some other set of rights. Even if it were clear what rights were being addressed it would be questionable whether the individual social worker is in a position to safeguard these. Although the social worker can act as advocate in obtaining for her 'relatively powerless' clients the rights and benefits to which they are entitled when some system already exists to furnish these, she is not in a position alone to create the means for ensuring that people receive their rights. She can assist clients in negotiating for benefits from the DHSS to which they are legally entitled; she cannot ensure that they are housed appropriately if adequate council housing is not available. She can press for facilities to be provided for individual clients or even for a whole client group, say the mentally ill; she is not in a position to make the policy decisions necessary to provide these.

What can it mean to say that the social worker should safeguard her clients' responsibility? The sense of responsibility that is intended here cannot be accountability, unless what is meant is that social workers should ensure that clients are held accountable for their actions. Of course at times social workers are involved in drawing the attention of clients to their accountability, for example in relation to parents who are known to neglect their children. However, drawing a client's attention to his accountability for his actions or omissions in relation to his children may not be what the Code intends here. Perhaps what is intended is some kind of 'personal responsibility'. Being responsible for one's life in the sense of making decisions about it is part of what constitutes human dignity and allows one to express one's individuality. Responsibility in this sense is very close in meaning to 'power' in that realising, or accepting, that we have responsibility for our lives allows us to exercise power over them. By encouraging and confirming clients' power over their lives social workers can indeed respect them as individuals and safeguard their dignity and responsibility for themselves.

Responsibility as choice

One way of encouraging and assisting clients to take responsibility for their lives is by helping them to realise and embrace choices. The choices that are open to an individual are constrained by factors such as wealth, intellectual level, health, status, personal power and the environment in which he lives. Although he is able to influence some of these factors, others may be totally outwith his control. However, each person has some choices open to him which allow him to exert some power or influence over his life. The extent to which a person is aware of, and able to make, choices, can be increased (and sometimes decreased) by processes such as education, psychotherapy, medical diagnosis and treatment, and social work intervention. The Code recognises this and states that the social worker 'will help his [her] clients increase the range of choices open to them and their powers to make decisions' (Principles of Practice, para. 10.4). By actively facilitating and encouraging recognition and acceptance of personal responsibility for choices made, social workers will be concerned not only with ensuring that their clients' responsibility in this sense is safeguarded but also with helping them to grow as responsible persons. The Code recognises that at times it is 'necessary to help the client to abandon pseudo- or fantasy choices so that effective choices may be made' (Commentary on Principles, para. 4). An example might be the frail elderly lady, newly discharged from hospital, who is bedridden and yet refuses domiciliary services such as home help or meals on wheels. Another would be a person, about to be evicted, who maintains that he cannot be forced to leave his home and that he intends to remain.

An individual's choices are made public in his actions and also in his omissions to act. He is personally responsible for the choices that he makes even when these do not result in action. For example a man who decides to have his hair cut before going for an interview is responsible for any consequences which follow from his choice to look smart; but he would also have been responsible for the consequences had he not had it cut because he had chosen to leave it long.

At times a person may allow things to happen to him, as object, rather than choosing, as agent, to influence things to the extent that he is able. Such 'allowings' are choices of a kind since they represent the choice to allow things to happen. Individuals are responsible for such choices, but they are to be distinguished from active participation in life and the *taking* of responsibility for oneself in the world.

Paul Watzlawick, who sees all of human behaviour as communication, writes that 'One cannot not communicate' (Watzlawick *et al.*, 1967); similarly one cannot not be responsible (in a causal sense) for one's actions and omissions to act, because one initiates them and is their cause. However, when the Code talks about safeguarding the client's responsibility, I think the intention is to refer to the client's ability and desire to accept personal responsibility for his life and to use this responsibility positively to influence his life and lifestyle.

Denying responsibility and choice

It is not uncommon for those who become clients of caring agencies to deny the responsibility they have for themselves and the course of their lives. One way in which they can do this is by denying that they have choices by which they can affect their lives. For example, a person who has been diagnosed as suffering from mental illness and who believes in this diagnosis may deny that she can do certain things or avoid doing certain others, claiming that her illness causes her to behave in certain ways and prevents her from behaving in others. In this way a person who has been diagnosed as suffering from a compulsive-obsessional neurosis might claim that her tendency to check and re-check what others are saying is the result of her illness rather than her lack of attention to what people are saying. The denial of responsibility is frequently found in social work practice, as when a client claims that she cannot do something when really she means that she will not do it because for some reason she has decided not to do so. For example, a woman may claim that she cannot leave her husband when really she means that despite the inconvenience and distress it causes her, she would rather stay with him than suffer the alternative. And a man may claim that he cannot do without his beer and tobacco in order to allow enough money to pay the rent arrears when really he means that he does not want to do this.

The offloading of responsibility for self and for choices made seems contrary to personal growth. Earlier I said that I take the Code's requirement that social workers accept a responsibility to facilitate the self-realisation of clients to be about helping them to grow in autonomy and personal responsibility. If the social worker is to make the personal growth of clients one of her professional concerns, therefore, she must become aware of those occasions when clients either consciously or unconsciously give up or deny responsibility for themselves. Among other things she may pay attention to the language in which her clients describe their situations to her. Much offloading of personal responsibility is embodied in statements such as 'It's always like this', 'Things are getting worse', 'Something's got to happen' and 'Someone will have to do something'. A social worker who accepts these as straightforward accounts of the situation, who passively allows the client to totally locate responsibility outside himself, will in many instances be giving the client 'permission' to deny his potential to act upon his problems. Allowing a client to deny his ability to make decisions about his own life, however bad the alternatives might be, is to encourage him to give up responsibility for himself.[2]

Responsibility and the client in residential care

Earlier I discussed some negative effects that might arise if accountability is construed in terms of the possibility of being blamed if things go wrong. I want now to focus that earlier discussion on the field of residential care. In particular I want to consider the extent to which clients in residential establishments are given the opportunity to be responsible for themselves.

Social workers in residential care who lay excessive stress on their accountability for the care of clients are likely to spend much of their time ensuring that clients are physically well rather than in encouraging them to take whatever responsibility for themselves they are capable of, in the sense of exercising whatever powers to make decisions they have.

There may be a tendency to overprotect to the detriment of the quality of life of residents in establishments caring for the elderly, the mentally handicapped and so on. Constraints placed upon behaviour can limit the extent to which clients can express and have their individuality as persons confirmed, in the residential setting. Society at large is more concerned with the physical state of those being cared for in residential establishments than with their psychological state. The reason for this might be that it is easier to notice the effects of physical ill-treatment or lack of care than it is to notice corresponding psychological effects. As a result caring establishments may emphasise physical rather than, and even at the expense of, emotional or spiritual welfare. This concern with physical well-being, while laudable, is perhaps paradoxical in the case of those who are being cared for primarily because of some degree of emotional or psychological disturbance, or because of mental handicap or infirmity.

In residential establishments, perhaps particularly those which care for the very old and the physically and mentally handicapped, it is not uncommon for virtually all responsibility to be taken away from residents. The way in which time is spent, hours of rising and going to bed, the food that is eaten and the ways in which residents relate to one another, may all be largely dictated by staff. In his book *Social Therapy in Psychiatry* (1974), David Clark implies that the removal of responsibility often happens for reasons of convenience. However, the removal of responsibility from clients may result from the attempt to make the physical environment and the activities that take place within it as safe as possible. For example, on a long-stay psychiatric ward or in an elderly person's home dealing with fragile clients, residents may be denied the opportunity to make cups of tea because of the risk of injury from boiling water. To the extent that they are denied the opportunity to engage in everyday activities such as this, residents are denied the right to exercise power over their own lives and the opportunity to take responsibility for their own welfare. Clark's comments are directed at psychiatry but they have relevance for social workers in both field and residential settings. He writes: 'Doctors and nurses are highly skilled at removing an individual's responsibility . . . . In general people are more ready for responsibilities than doctors and nurses credit . . . many nurses and doctors only too readily think: it would be done better and quicker if I do it myself.'

The tendency of practitioners in residential establishments to view their responsibility in terms of accountability may thus result in the erosion of the responsibility of clients in such establishments. To the extent that responsibility is removed from the individual in care, his ability to help in the process of his own 'healing' or 'growing' or 'treatment' (in establishments where this is an aim), or to take his being as a person as fully as possible, will be diminished. At times encouraging the responsibility of clients will conflict with the task of caring for their physical welfare. Risks may have to be taken in allowing clients who have limited ability to care for themselves to take the little responsibility of which they are capable. Very psychologically disturbed or extremely mentally or physically handicapped people may have limited capacity for responsibility. However, even in such cases it is only by encouraging responsibility for self that the individuals concerned can be helped to live their lives to the fullest possible extent. As Clark says in the continuation of my earlier quotation from him, 'it may be far more helpful to [the client] to exercise his own responsibility, make his own mistakes, surmount his difficulties and grow a little.' The fact that a person has extremely limited intellectual or physical ability does not necessarily mean that we must do everything for him, that he is thereby incapable of taking responsibility for himself. Rather it means that in facilitating his capacity to choose we must look very carefully for those areas of his life in which he is capable of taking responsibility and then afford him the opportunity to be responsible in those areas. A very physically handicapped man may not be able to wash, dress, feed or toilet himself but that does not mean that he is incapable of choosing the food that he eats; and although a mentally handicapped man may not be capable of performing complex tasks on his own, he may be able to assist with them even though they might take more time and be less efficiently done when he does so.

Of course it is not just in the residential setting that there is the temptation to remove the responsibility of clients. Field workers will be familiar with the experience of thinking that, for example, it would be easier to sort out a client's financial difficulties oneself than to support the client in the attempt to do so. The desire to succeed in helping clients, and the desire to appear efficient to one's colleagues and the world, may at times lead us to take over tasks that would be better left to the client. This is not to safeguard the client's responsibility.

At times safeguarding a client's responsibility may conflict with the social worker's 'responsibility to help clients to obtain all those services and rights to which they are entitled both from the agency in which he works and from any other source' (Principles of Practice, para. 10.10). Since 'Social workers are often at the interface between powerful organisations and relatively powerless applicants for services' (Statement of Principles, para. 9), it will often be appropriate for them to assist in ensuring that clients receive assistance to which they are entitled. However, this will not always be the case. For example, where clients are capable of negotiating their own entitlements but are unmotivated to do so, assistance may erode the client's capacity to determine his own affairs. The social worker's dilemma is in striking a balance between helping as an advocate and encouraging the client to take the responsibility for his life that he is able to.

A second conflict is worth noting here, that between the social worker's responsibility to her client and to her agency. Her responsibility to ensure that clients receive the 'services and rights' to which they are entitled may involve her acting against the agency of which she is an employee at times, if she considers that it does not provide for these entitlements to be fulfilled. Indeed the Code, recognising that the social worker cannot always fulfil his responsibilities 'for relief and prevention of hardship and suffering . . . by direct service to individual families and groups' (Statement of Principles, para. 9) asserts that the social worker 'has the right and duty to bring to the attention of those in power, and of the general public, ways in which the activities of government, society or agencies, create or contribute to hardship and suffering or militate against their relief' (Statement of Principles, para. 9). In pursuing this 'right and duty' it may well be that the social worker will be forced to enter into dispute with her own agency and the local authority which funds it. Such conflicts are further examined in the chapters by Malcolm Payne and Huw Richards.

5   The Code of Ethics, the social work manager and the organisation

Malcolm Payne

Introduction

There is controversy about whether social work can be regarded as a profession and proposing a code of ethics fuels that controversy in various ways. One argument which may support the view that social work is not a profession is that it is almost always practised within organisations and social workers are usually more subject to the authority of their employers rather than being directly accountable to clients for their decisions. A code of ethics is based in the idea of personal professional responsibility to clients, so how can it be squared with responsibility to an employer? This paper examines some aspects of this problem which arise in the BASW Code.

The problem is recognised in the Code by saying (para. 3) that the social workers are responsible to clients, employers, each other, professional colleagues and society, and by the statement of the Commentary (para. 4) that it is an oversimplification to say that either clients or employers should take precedence. Although it is clear on the nature of the possibly conflicting responsibilities, by refusing to give guidance on *balancing* them against one another, the Code is inadequate as a guide (even generalised) to practice, although its existence might inform clients, if they knew about it, of ways in which they might protect themselves. The view that these responsibilities can be equal in importance is certainly different from the stance taken in paragraph 1, that the 'primary objective of the Code' is to prescribe rules 'for the protection of clients'. This seems to suggest that they should take priority over employers.

Is this a real conflict? In the next section, I shall show that it is an important and difficult issue for social workers and that it comes up again and again. Furthermore, I argue that the Code offers little in the way of helpful guidance; paragraphs dealing with matters of concern to employers are vague and generally do not deal with employers' worries.

Why do the conflicts arise? I argue that an important characteristic of organisations is that they are instruments for distributing and employing power. A number of facts must be borne in mind in considering a Code designed to protect clients. First, the most powerful groups in state organisations often have interests at variance with the clients, who are of a different and disadvantaged social class and cultural background. Second, organisations for social welfare are guided by policies which are considered (by the powerful groups in society who carry them into practice) to be for the general good, or are presented as being for the general good. Such a good may conflict with the good of particular individuals or groups in society. Third, people in organisations have a tendency to seek to maintain the power and influence of the organisation, and their interests in doing so often conflict with the interests of the organisation's clients.

Having looked at these problems and how they affect social workers, in the following section of the paper I discuss the position of managers. First, if they are social workers, are there any issues which arise for them as signatories to the Code in carrying out their duties as managers when they also have a duty to act representing the powers and interests of the agency? Second, as managers of social workers, is there any way they can act to help deal with the problems of agency-ethical conflict in their role as representatives of the agency's interests? Finally, I shall try to suggest some guidelines for applying the Code which may help to solve some of these problems in ways which I consider to be ethical, but having reasonable regard for employers' interests, and so recognising the problem of divided loyalties.

The Code and social work in an organisation

Social workers trying to put their clients' interests first, and to treat their clients as self-responsible and with dignity, come up against the interests of their agency, since according to the Code they must always have regard to their responsibility to their agency. Moreover, social workers are in a relatively powerless position in the agency's power structure. However much they argue, they are employees, and must obey their superiors in the end; they are usually less well-informed than their superiors; they have very restricted power to command resources, other than their own time. So, even where there is professional agreement about the proper behaviour in the client's interests, the power of the agency may be used to enforce the agency's interests. And because of its generalised interests in wider social benefits than those of individual clients, representatives of agency interests also represent the interests of the whole client group as opposed to individuals, and society's good. An integral part of this problem is the political nature of control of many agencies. If the final decision is in political hands, professional decisions often lose their validity when controversial matters arise because matters with moral overtones or resource implications are felt to be the province of politicans rather than relatively junior staff. What is ethical behaviour, then, becomes very unclear.

Case One is an example of this process. Mr Andrews had a physically handicapped son, and sought to borrow an area office's reference books for available aids and adaptations. This was refused on the grounds that the social services department could not provide all the aids he might gain advantage from; it had a public duty to ration government expenditure wisely. Further, in the client's interests, it was argued that he might be disappointed and frustrated, by later refusal, and that he would be unable to make the best professional decision about the most appropriate aid. In a situation where he might already be under considerable stress, through caring for his son, and had very strong feelings of duty to provide the best for him, additional emotional stress should be avoided. Choosing the wrong aid could lead to discomfort, perhaps actual physical harm, to this son.

The social worker, attending to the BASW Code's Statement of Principles, can argue that it enhances the client's human dignity, individuality and responsibility (paras. 6 and 10.2) to be open, that she has a duty to 'help clients increase the range of choices open to them and their powers to make decisions' (paragraph 10.4) and help clients get all their rights (para 10.10). It clearly demonstrates a greater respect for Mr Andrews's parental responsibility for his handicapped child; it allows him to make choices which suit the particular needs of his child, needs he knows better than an occasional visiting social worker, and it allows him to test out his decisions against the fullest information available and to gain reassurance from having done so. His knowledge of the detail of home life might allow him to see opportunities for aids to be used which might not be seen by a visitor not living with his son.

The agency on the other hand may have a strong interest in not incurring a greater expenditure. On their representative's side is the public policy duty to restrain expenditure. The advisability of total disclosure can also be questioned: in general a guided choice may be better than the confusion of fuller information. Further, a client's rights might arguably be better safeguarded by professional, informed decisions about the child's needs. While Mr Andrews gains the freedom to make his own decisions, it is possible these may not be in the best interests of the child. One important piece of guidance which the Code gives is the commentary on paragraph 4 which suggests that agencies should allow social workers the right to exercise professional discretion. Such discretion derives from a specialised education and experience which is assumed to fit a qualified worker to be more flexible in decision-making than a bureaucrat whose decisions must be more closely confined by rules. So if the social worker offers help to Mr Andrews and judges that in this particular case the client has the character and intelligence to make sensible choices and not be frustrated by the lack of resources, her discretion should prevail. Against this, the agency can put the public policy advantage of non-disclosure of the information; its construction of the client's interests; and also can argue that a precedent may be created which might later disadvantage other clients.

Case Two, Bert Baines, was a 15-year-old living in a council estate where there was delinquency, truancy and vandalism. He was absent from school for much of the last year, was in care but home on trial because of an offence committed a few years ago. The education welfare officer wanted Bert taken into residential care because, he argued, Bert's immunity from removal encouraged other children to disbelieve the sanctions which exist against truancy. Bert's father ran a successful, if informal, car repair business and Bert wanted to follow him. Much of Bert's time was spent tinkering with cars and learning the trade informally. He and his father believed that this would be more use to him than school work, not unreasonably since the school provided no technical subjects. The school shared the education welfare officer's enthusiasm for Bert's removal explicitly to deter others from following Bert's example and recognised that they could offer him little. Bert's younger brother, at 13, regularly attended school and the social worker thought that if Bert's influence on the neighbourhood was so malign it could be expected to influence his brother most: this indicated that fear of Bert's example to the others was not supported by the evidence. The education department put pressure on the social services department which feared the loss of co-operation in other cases, or that political dispute in the Council Chamber might also stir up public opinion against the agency. It was also argued that, even if Bert and his father disagreed, school and a good school record would benefit any child.

In these cases, three main points have arisen:

1 The client's best interests were uncertain and the agency's representatives could interpret those interests to fit the agency's wishes.

2 The alleged interests of the generality of clients, and the community at large, can often be interpreted to support the agency's concern for maintaining its own position.

3 The social worker's 'right to professional discretion' is not powerful on behalf of clients' interests against these advantages of the agency because the factual basis of the discretion is open to dispute.

In addition to these points about the reality of the social worker's position in a dispute with the agency, there are a number of aspects of the Code itself which strengthen the agency's defence of other interests than those of the client in any particular case.

The first of these is the duty to co-operate with others (paras. 8 and 10.8). In each case already discussed, this was a consideration which the agency quoted against what the social worker took to be the client's interest. Cases Three and Four are further examples where this is the major issue.

Case Three, Mrs Cornhill, was an elderly lady whose husband had just died and who was unable to care for herself. Her family doctor asked the social services department to arrange admission to an old people's home. When the doctor applied pressure to her she agreed to go, but when the social worker asked, more neutrally, she refused. The doctor felt that pressure was appropriate because care in her home was inadequate and she needed admission. The social worker felt that this approach unethically denied Mrs Cornhill's right to decide, but co-operation on this and other cases was threatened. While, of course, co-operation at any price should not be required, the agency has a greater interest in maintaining such co-operation for the benefit of all than in damaging it by maintaining the right of only one client whose interests were not seriously damaged in other ways.

Case Four, Doris Dowland, was a hyperactive child in a children's home who was very disruptive. The home's doctor, when called, prescribed large doses of largactil, a major tranquiliser, to reduce her hyperactivity, but staff refused to give this sedation because they felt it reduced Doris's 'dignity, individuality, rights and responsibility' as the Code puts it. Such heavy medication would reduce her capacity to enjoy life actively, reduce her capacity to think and feel, and prevent her from trying to learn to control her own behaviour. It was no long-term answer, since sooner or later she must learn self-control and drugging prevents a start being made on that process. The doctor, called out two or three times to deal with the injuries of other children caused by her violence, refused to come out again unless the medication was given as prescribed.

In both these cases, senior managers in the agency supported the doctors' sides against what social workers took to be the interests of the clients, arguing that the maintenance of co-operation was more important for the generality of clients than the interests of these particular clients.

It might be argued that paragraph 10.8 only requires co-operation where it is in the interests of clients but this does not help to defend the interests of a particular client against the view that the interests of the generality of clients lie in maintaining co-operation; and again the power of the agency's apparatus tends to be in favour of collaboration rather than conflict. The assumption of paragraph 10.8 that collaboration is in the interests of clients, then, may be reasonable in general, but may not work out in individual cases.

A number of points arise from these cases about the nature of the interests which are under consideration. The interests which were claimed on either side were often quite speculative; what actually would be in the interests of each client or of the generality of others is factually uncertain and certainly could be misconstrued. How, then, can we characterise the client's interest? Barry (1964) proposes that something is in our interest only if it increases our opportunities to get what we want. This approach fits particularly well with the importance the Code attaches to increasing the range of choice available to a client. It is not the whole answer, however, because clients, like anyone else, may be wrong about what they want, or about the best way of attaining it. This often gives a professional with experience of many similar circumstances a strength behind his view of what is best for a client, and it gives some force to the speculations which have been presented here: they are based on an assumed familiarity with, and learning about, what is to the client a new and unusual experience. It is also hard to decide how the individual interest of the client can be judged against the general interests of the public. Here, Barry proposes that we should accept as in the public interest only 'what measure will benefit me in common with everyone else rather than one at the expense of everyone else'. From this idea of Rousseau, he suggests that it is sometimes possible to arrive at a 'net benefit': sometimes the advantage of others outweighs the client's loss, sometimes not.

The second aspect of the Code which adds to the social worker's difficulties in using it against agency interests in favour of the client's interests is the way in which the Code deals with *the duty of involvement in policy-making and public knowledge*. Paragraph 9 requires social workers to 'bring to the attention of those in power and of the general public ways in which the activities of government, society or agencies create or contribute to hardship and suffering or militate against their relief'. The Commentary emphasises that, although there is a responsibility to employers in doing this, the client's 'lack of power must be taken into account in weighing these responsibilities'. The implication of this is that social workers must make special efforts to reveal injustices affecting the least powerful.

A number of practical problems are raised by these parts of the Code. It is not clear how social workers know that they have discharged their duty to bring something to the attention of those in power and the public. Is writing a memorandum to their superior enough? Or should they get together and publish a report? When do they give up on those in power and go for the general public? And, in order to reach the general public, are they entitled to go on demonstrations, or publicise their case on radio and television? It must be remembered that they have a duty to do this in order to expose the activities of their employing agencies, which might not be too happy about such action. Those in power and the general public may take no notice and carry on acting to create hardship. Having said this, either loudly or softly, is the duty discharged, or must social workers carry on bringing to attention these activities until they achieve change? Presumably it must be the latter, because otherwise the hardship would continue and so would the duty to bring to attention. In which case, it seems, a social worker has a moral duty to decide what changes are required and to continue to seek them. Although this is not explicitly required by the Code, it seems to be implied by the consequences of unsuccessful 'bringing to attention'. Singer (1973) provides some help here. He argues that 'disobedience' can be a morally acceptable (and effective) way of obtaining a fair hearing or having a situation recognised by those in authority. He proposes that clear limits are set to such disobedience if it takes place in a democracy in which attempts to persuade of the wisdom of a change of policy are permissible, and attempts to enforce it by deviousness or violence are not. Thus, he would propose that the social worker should only use enough disobedience to *present* the case to the public, that it should not be coercive or intimidating. He also suggests that the constant projection of one point of view is not justified: once it is 'brought to attention', the duty has been fulfilled, even though others are unpersuaded.

The second practical problem is the emphasis on power and powerlessness as the determinant of action. Where the client appears relatively powerless to affect decisions about his/her life compared with the agency, the client's rights and satisfying his/her needs have priority. Agencies are powerful because power is concentrated by and in certain kinds of social structure; in social classes, in formal organisations, in limitations on the availability of knowledge, for instance. Such patterns of power are strongly institutionalised, not least in the staffing structure of agencies where social workers occupy relatively powerless positions themselves. Power over others also exists because people are in the habit of treating certain groups or organisations as powerful, whether or not in any particular case they have the resources to impose their wishes. The fact of working, therefore, in a formal organisation, of being part of government and of being part of a class structure which gives advantages to professionals, creates a situation whereby social workers and their agencies have and maintain considerable power over groups in society from which most clients come. It is unrealistic to suppose that all this can be negated by a pallid injunction.

Paragraph 9 thus enjoins the social worker to act against policies and activities of the powerful, but fails to recognise that the realities of power constrain such action to the extent of making the requirement worthless. The effect of a paragraph requiring social workers only to 'bring to the attention' of the powerful and the public various injustices and to be 'accountable to those under whose authority they work' is that the agency's final authority is conceded by the Code.

Similar points can be made about a number of the Code's Principles of Practice. 10.1 requires a contribution to policy-making, and avoiding inhuman policies; but the final recourse offered is merely resignation. 10.2 requires the safeguarding of clients' dignity, individuality, rights and responsibility, but I have argued already that these are very difficult to maintain against agency commitments. 10.3 requires the social worker not to act selectively towards clients on grounds of various forms of prejudice. However, all social work agencies operate selectively and demean by taking away personal responsibility and by disadvantaging many groups. Such groups are mainly those against which there is often prejudice. It could therefore be argued that social work agencies have prejudice built into their existence. It is widely recognised that social work in the United Kingdom is largely a service for those of low social status (Jordan, 1979); women have been disadvantaged in their treatment by the social services (e.g. battered wives; in the lack of provision of nursery facilities to enable them to work); the elderly have been widely disadvantaged by ageism – the assumption that they are unable to care for themselves (Marshall, 1983); and there is still prejudice in favour of the 'deserving' in social services; in other words, better treatment because of a 'contribution to society'. The way these attitudes are an integral part of the provision of social services as they are organised in the United Kingdom presses any social worker who is part of an agency to act selectively in these ways, and such unjustified selectivity enforces prejudiced behaviour.

10.5 obliges social workers not to reject their clients, but also assumes an obligation to protect others against them. This again leads to difficulties in the social worker's relationship with the agency, because the agency's concern with general social and public policy will raise the duty to protect against the particular interest of any client. The following cases are examples.

In *Case Five*, Mr and Mrs Eagleton applied to become foster-parents and were found on investigation to be satisfactory in every way, until Mr Eagleton's police record was discovered to contain a sentence of Borstal training more than twenty years previously for an indecent assault. Although this was a long way in the past and everyone in the social services department felt that the Eagletons would be successful foster-parents, they were rejected because of fears of the public reaction should something go wrong in the future, and the conviction be publicly revealed. Here (taking the Eagletons as clients) the clients' interests were sacrificed for the agency's public image and on the grounds of being seen to fulfil the duty to protect. In this instance, the agency (and the social worker) is forced to compromise with unreasonable arguments because of the distribution of power. The need to compromise in this way derives from the importance of retaining the agency's credibility. Thus, in order to implement a social work service through a state agency, events almost inevitably arise which place in opposition the social worker's service to his clients and the agency's commitment to policies which justify its power.

In *Case Six*, Felicity Fielding was a 15-year-old girl in care while her mother was homeless, following marital difficulties. Eventually, the mother found a suitable home, but it was discovered that she had been warned by the police for prostitution. Again, public reaction was feared by the social services department if Felicity was returned home on trial and the mother's occupation revealed, in court for example. Even though care at home was likely to be excellent, and both mother and daughter wished to be reunited, the protection argument was again used to defend the agency's advantage. In such a case the argument may not seem convincing to an outsider but party political involvement in social services departments has occasionally invested cases of this kind with overtones which make the 'best interests of the child' arguments hard to maintain even when superior.

10.7 is mainly concerned with social workers' responsibilities for continuing their professional education and development, but the final section holds the social worker 'responsible for the standard of service he gives'. The commentary says that this 'is crucial to professionalism. A completely bureaucratised service cannot be a professional one.' Obviously, in such an activity as social work, if agencies sought to prescribe every act of social workers, it would be impossible for both to work well. This requirement is, however, absolute. What happens if the agency does not organise itself efficiently, or indeed creates disadvantages and will not respond to social workers' efforts to change it? Does the social worker still have to accept responsibility for the standard of service? In my view, this is unreasonable and the Code should recognise the agency's at least partial responsibility for the standard of service. This, of course, is a strong basis for 'bringing to attention' circumstances where responsibilities cannot be met because of agency failures. It is often hard to do this, however, because such arguments about resources come down to political choices and social workers may be perceived as making inappropriate political comments. The Code of Practice in Child Abuse Cases (BASW, 1975b) recognises the agency's responsibility to provide an adequate level of support and resources, and the report of the Working Party on client participation (BASW, 1980) also stresses the agency's responsibility. It may be that paragraph 10.12 is relevant here, since it requires social workers to work for conditions in their agency which allow them to accept the obligations of the Code. This puts the obligations on the social workers but implies a requirement also on the agency for the appropriate conditions.

10.9 bears centrally on how some workers deal in practice with their duty to reveal to the general public policies which disadvantage clients. It suggests how a social worker should behave when acting publicly. 'He will make clear in making public statements or undertaking any public activities, whether he is acting in a personal capacity, or on behalf of an organisation.' The implications of this, from the point of view of an agency, are that a social worker should not purport to represent it unless authorised to do so.

Again, however, there are serious practical problems in interpreting this requirement. What is a public statement? Is a discussion in a local public house, overheard by a councillor, a public statement? Is a revelation on a training course designed to help staff deal with problems, but which leads to rumour and innuendo, a public statement? Is participation in a meeting limited to social workers a public statement? Is participation in a meeting including other professionals such as teachers and doctors a public statement? Is a comment to the press designed to cool a situation and made 'off the record' but quoted by the press in any event a public statement? How do social workers *make clear* the organisations they represent? Will this be readily understood or even listened to by press? While social workers may not be responsible if they are misinterpreted, they may be held responsible by their agency.

Even if social workers make clear in criticising their agency that they are acting personally or representing another organisation, such as a professional association, the power of criticism derives from the fact that a social worker is a member of the agency and a professional and therefore may be presumed to know something about it. Here are three examples.

In *Case Seven* the warden of a sheltered housing scheme was employed by the social services department and was also chairman of the local residents' association and a leader in the local community. She made a speech as chairman of the association at one of its meetings criticising some social services department policies for the elderly as it applied to local residents. The press report quoted her job as well as her office with the association. The social services department delivered an informal warning against this behaviour, feeling that an employee of the department should not, as such, be associated with criticism of it. The warden, of course, suffered from a conflict of interests, but her position as an employee was regarded *by the agency* which had the power to discipline her as the paramount interest which she should respect.

In *Case Eight* a social worker, feeling that clients had been unreasonably evicted from their home by the local authority housing department, rang the newspaper to seek publicity for the case and was quoted as making critical comments of the local authority. He was reprimanded.

In a similar case, *Case Nine*, the social worker arranged for a reporter to be present at the eviction hearing at the County Court, and briefed the reporter privately. Although there was a considerable furore, her part in it was not known.

In the housing cases, the results – a stay of eviction – were rather similar; and in both cases the social worker brought to the attention of the general public the unsatisfactory policies. One was reprimanded, and the other was not; was the latter rewarded for deviousness or circumspection? Singer (1973) would suggest that it is better, in a democracy, when disobeying in order to draw attention to an injustice, to own up and accept punishment, partly because it demonstrates that you accept the right of superiors to discipline you for transgressing. In these cases, however, there are further points on either side. The social workers (and warden) who sought or received publicity for criticisms of the local authority might reasonably claim the ineffectiveness of internal represent-ations, and that the local authority has no real systems for dealing with conflicts of policy: what is usually required is obedience and ineffective internal comment. On the other hand, the local authority can reasonably claim that the relevant decision-makers were unaware of the views before they became public, and internal representations, ineffective as they may be, had not been attempted. Another point is that the local authority can claim that its actions in the housing cases were legal and generally supported by public antipathy to people who failed to pay rent. In reply to this, the social workers can claim that what is legal is not always right or the most effective way to handle the situation. It can also be claimed that they have the right to try to change the public conception of what is right, by presenting information or argument about the damage caused (for example to children) by a policy of frequent eviction.

Clearly, in any case, there are serious difficulties in making public one's views. This can even be so when doing it privately to people responsible for the service, as the next case shows.

In *Case Ten*, during a period of financial restraint, it was decided not to replace any staff who left. A warden who visited elderly people daily to see whether they were well, resigned: her visits were reallocated to other staff, but a few clients had their service withdrawn. Recognising that the changes might lead to problems, the area officer wrote to local councillors telling them of the arrangements and agreeing to look at them again if representations were made to them on behalf of clients. The letter contained a phrase regretting that some clients from whom the service was withdrawn would be more at risk. This letter was discussed at the social services committee and led to a motion by a local councillor that no action by the social services department should ever place anyone at risk. Although this motion was – narrowly – defeated, and it was recognised that the letter was courteous and helpful to councillors, the officer was none the less reprimanded by order of the committee for writing such a statement in such a way.

In general then, I argue that the Code gives little clear practical guidance on how individual ethical requirements can be met in employment in structured organisations. While requiring adherence to obligations towards the client, the Code usually implies that conflicting obligations to the agency must be equally or more important. I have tried to show that the agency's position is usually such that it will have significant power to gain control of these conflicts in order to protect its political position and its institutionalised status.

How does this affect the position of managers of social workers? Does it cause them further difficulties? Can they help to resolve the social workers' problems? These are the subjects of the next section.

The social work manager and the Code

The Code presents two different kinds of problem for social work managers. First, they are themselves usually social workers and they face some of the problems of complying with it. Second, they act as representatives and interpreters of agency policy when supervising and directing social workers and so they are faced directly with trying to resolve conflicts between the Code and agency policy or requirements.

The manager as signatory to the Code

The major problem for managers as signatories to the Code is that they are responsible for social workers, yet the Code is set down in terms of the needs of clients. This creates a problem of divided loyalties. Are managers' duties to staff to take second place to the needs of clients? Or are managers to treat social workers as in effect their clients and apply the Code substituting 'social worker' for 'client'? Or are they entitled to ignore all but the general provisions of the Code as not applying to them?

All of these three approaches seem inappropriate separately and I would argue that each must play a part in the manager's concern for ethical behaviour. Managers cannot always place staff second to clients because a direct part of their work is to support staff and their personal development. Neither are social workers clients: they are independent professionals who must take responsibility for their work; they are not seeking help. And managers cannot ignore the importance of the parts of the Code which are of direct, detailed import to the relationships between clients and social workers, and they must take these into account. Many managers are used by social workers as models for appropriate behaviour and therefore need to take care that it is ethical.

A helpful balance which managers can undertake between these approaches to their positions as signatories to the Code might therefore be as follows:

1   The manager in making decisions about clients should always behave ethically under the Code, even though the decision may only have effect at one remove and he/she has no direct contact with the client.

2   The manager, when making decisions about situations where clients' needs conflict with those of staff, should act bearing in mind the broader concerns expressed in the Code in requirements for the development of policy, professional education, collaboration and professional discretion. Here, the commentary on Principle 10.6 is important: 'It does not imply that at all times the social worker must put his responsibility to a client above his other responsibilities, for example, as a citizen, as a parent.'

3   The manager should accept a particular responsibility to contribute to the broader aims of the Code, using the wider view of social work received in his/her position.

4   The manager should apply the standard of ethical behaviour required by the Code in relation to the rights of individuals (e.g. 10.2, 10.3, 10.4) to his/her staff.

The manager as agency representative

It is as an agency representative that the manager comes most into contact with the conflicts identified in the Code. In discussion of the difficulties which arose in the conflict between the client's interests and those of the agency, I identified four reasons to maintain the client's interest. Is there any way in which a manager can help to resolve these conflicts?

1 Uncertainty about the client's best interests

Where such uncertainty exists, it would help if the manager took responsibility for ensuring that there was as much clear evidence of the client's wishes, capacities and situation as bears on the problem. In Case One (rationing the disabled), the capacity of Mr Andrews to handle the information and the availability of the social worker to help might be relevant deciding factors and clear information might strengthen the client's position. Managers can also assist, from a relatively neutral stance, in deciding the 'net interest' from balancing public and an individual client's interests.

2 The agency's reputation and relationships

Where these are threatened, it would help if the manager took responsibility for trying to maintain the reputation and relationships by emphasising their strengths and past successes, and demonstrating the individual nature of the present problem being handled by the social worker (without blaming the social worker). Stressing the right to professional disagreement, and the general common interest, might help. If the social worker is in conflict with the agency for such reasons, the manager should take responsibility for overruling an ethical duty by issuing a clear direction, and if this is not enough to overcome the social worker's scruples, the manager should act, with no detriment to the social worker's position in the agency.

3 The general interests of other clients, community or public policy

Here, the manager can help by ensuring that the conflict of interests is clearly identified and explained to the client; the manager can also explore whether alternative services or actions will help the client, and whether an exception can be made which will maintain the general interest while protecting the client's needs. In this way, responsibility is still accepted for the general interest, but responsibility is also taken for helping the client find ways round these problems at a higher level in the agency than the social worker.

4   Strengthening professional discretion

The manager can strengthen the social worker's position by assessing the evidence and judgment on which the decision is based and adding the manager's influence to it. Thus, the social worker's discretion is strengthened by the manager's more powerful discretion. The manager also has a rather different range of responsibilities and knowledge and can see a broader picture which gives him also a different basis for his/her discretion.

These approaches are practical ways of using the manager's position to strengthen the position of the social worker when faced with ethical conflicts with the agency's interests, and they do not comprise the agency's position. They do not seem a particularly strong way of dealing with the conflicts, however, and it would seem useful to back them up with some further principles for dealing with conflicts between the Code and agency commitments.

Some further principles for dealing with Code–agency conflicts

In Case One, the problem of the agency's need to ration resources arose: it does seem wrong to ration by secrecy and so perhaps the client should have the right to know what services and facilities might be provided by social workers, given in a way and with such personal assistance as is necessary to enable the client to act on the information in accordance with his wishes. At the same time, information should be provided about the restrictions on resources so that the client is aware of the likely results of the decisions made. If, then, the service cannot be provided, an explanation can be made of the reasons for the decisions, including the criteria for setting priorities, because open, reasoned decisions often provide a better basis for consensus or compromise than closed, apparently irrational ones.

Another issue which arose in the first two cases was a conflict in the interpretation of what was in the client's best interests. There are two situations: first, where a client expresses a preference which the social worker can take into account, and second, where the social worker may have to consider rejecting such an expressed preference. The principle should be that where the client has expressed a preference, this should be regarded as having a stronger influence on a decision than any assumed benefits which might be inferred by the agency but whose validity is not accepted by the client, because clients are the best, but not the only, judge of their benefit because they are most aware of all the factors and particularly of the judgment of feeling what is best for them. Their judgment cannot be completely overriding, however, because they may be mistaken, or ignorant of how they can achieve what is in their interest, or be wrong about how they will feel about their needs when they achieve them.

In Case Two, Bert Baines was to have action taken against him which was admitted to be disadvantageous because it was thought to benefit others. In such cases, the client's expressed preference may appear to be at risk because of clear benefits to others which override the principle set out in the foregoing paragraph. The social worker's guiding principle should, even so, be that no action should be taken against a client which actually disadvantages him/her because of benefits received by others. Action which does not disadvantage the client, but is neutral in effect, would be acceptable. Any action which reduced contacts or the right to live with others of the client's choice, or restricted their freedom, should be regarded as disadvantaging a client. Thus direct benefits should be more important than general or indirect benefits – and no one should be a mere instrument in promoting others' welfare.

In other cases, the advantage to others was very general in nature. Another useful principle is that no action should be taken to the disadvantage of a client unless specific advantage or protection can be shown to benefit others directly as a result. Such a principle could apply to problems where the need to collaborate gets in the way of a client's interests. In Case Three, for example, it might be wrong to take the doctor's side because Mrs Cornhill's needs are the main issue; no others gain or lose. In Case Four, on the other hand, several people are affected by any problems in collaboration, and there is more of a balance of interests.

All the principles proposed here derive from the importance of the client's right to choice, dignity and independence, as far as it is possible to secure these.

The next range of issues which are discussed above concern the duty to take part in policy-making. Here, there is a clear responsibility to attempt to influence agency policy and to create or use machinery for doing so. If this fails, machinery could be used which is independent of the agency, which retains the duty of confidentiality of clients' personal information, and is administered by groups or individuals familiar with the issues and the organisation of relevant agencies. Thus, professional, trade union or multi-professional machinery might be appropriate. Use of the press or media in individual cases is of doubtful effectiveness and adds stresses to the client's problems, according to an experienced commentator, Harvey (1972), and so is only valid where it is *urgently* required, where the client demands it, or at least accedes to it, where other ways of placing the problem before the public are not available, and public pressure is required for a resolution. The Code is concerned with resolving policy issues through influencing the public, not resolving individual cases. So urgency, client demand, lack of alternatives, the necessity of publicity and the generality of the issues should be the criteria for publicity.

Endword

In this paper, I have tried to show how the Code fails to deal with the conflict of working in a social work agency and the assumed predominance of individual clients' interests. The important difficulty is the tendency of an institutionalised powerful agency with general interests of its own to use its power to promote its interests against the interests of individual clients. I have suggested that managers have a responsibility to help social workers deal with the politics of such conflicts without compromising their duties to the agency. I have also suggested some guidelines for applying the Code in such conflicts which may assist in resolving the difficulties.

6 Social work, professional social workers and the Code of Ethics

Huw Richards

Introduction

The British Association of Social Workers has produced and endorsed a Code of Ethics for those who are 'professionally' employed in social work. In this discussion I examine some reasons for extending the application of the Code. I consider ways in which it can be extended to inform a more extensive interpretation of social work as well as professional social work services to clients. I hope to show that in circumstances of scarce resources, and by the general nature of social caring, social workers' obligations set out in the Code of Ethics can be shared with other carers including clients. I illustrate the convergence of interests between social workers and clients by taking three categories of statements of client rights and entitlements, and show how the Code of Ethics leads to action by social workers and their clients informed by these sources.

The application of the Code

The limit of the Code of Ethics to 'professional activity' is stated in paragraph 1 of the Objectives. The Code is therefore a professionals' code. The efficacy of such codes of ethics is affected by several factors. First, a code's standing will be affected by the extent to which the activities to which it refers are an exhaustive description of professional social work. Second, the activities (fully described or otherwise) referred to in the Code may not be exclusively undertaken and performed by those to whom the Code is addressed. Third, a significantly large number of professional social workers have not agreed to be regulated by the Code in terms of any form of registration which could accompany endorsement of the Code. This has been noted by the British Association of Social Workers elsewhere: 'caring was not invented by social workers and we have neither the responsibility or the right to attempt to undertake it exclusively' (BASW, 1980). Clients, therefore, will want to know how 'defaulting' will be discovered and regulated, and how the aim of 'the protection of clients' is going to be achieved. If there are no sanctions to which the professional body of people are subject should they fail to act within its terms and spirit, the Code's status is considerably weakened. This in no way suggests that the content of the Code is inappropriate for professional social workers, but the limitation to professional workers is a considerable narrowing of its relevance without obvious benefits in its application to practice. If we examine the breadth of activity which might be called 'social work', and note some other participants in the enterprise, we may find that the Code has a broader relevance, in terms of its influence on values and practice, and can avoid creating insoluble problems of regulation.

Clearly even professional social work is not limited to the membership of the British Association of Social workers, neither can social work be usefully defined as Local Authority social work employment. To be 'providing a service' or being 'employed in caring' would also not provide a clear definition of social work to which the Code would apply. There are a number of people and functions which are distinguished from the normal activities of citizens and which fall within a broad notion of social work but which are not performed by professionally employed social workers. Is the Code of Ethics relevant for such actors as foster-parents, next-of-kin in cases of mental disorder, volunteers in social work settings, members of mutual aid and self-help groups, informal carers of the elderly, and also clients and patients? That 'social work is a professional activity' must be understood as a statement concerning *some* social work, to which the Code is addressed, rather than *all* social work. Furthermore, assertion that social work *is* a professional activity cannot be supported by evidence that social work is a self-regulating profession. The narrow application of the Code may therefore prevent the spread of values that could inform the activity of social caring and limit them to a particular group of people who happen to do professional social work. The reasons for not limiting the Code to professional social workers are practical and not a criticism of the content of the Code.

I am concerned with the extent of the useful application of the Code rather than the extent to which others not engaged in social work might agree with its principles. I therefore do not mean to suggest that most citizens do share or ought to share the obligations noted in the Code. The British Association of Social Workers, by providing a Code, has stated that there are certain obligations beyond those of the ordinary citizen and that there is something relatively uncommon in the 'special obligations' within social work. There are, after all, many citizens who in role or attitude exhibit indifference rather than compassion towards the clients of social services departments.

However, the group of 'carers' listed above would commonly endorse the Code and accept that they have special obligations. They may also wish to consider what their 'complementary rights' might be (Foreword, paragraph 4). For example, 'informal carers' looking after elderly confused relatives, or foster-parents who accept a variety of children, may wish to have a more active 'complementary right' to influence local social service policy in so far as it affects them.

One might still agree that a telling reason for a Code for 'professional social workers' is that they are distinguished from other 'carers' by the considerable extent of their professional discretion. However, checks upon the use of power and discretion which social workers possess to decide upon matters which directly affect the client's life may be better achieved by the use of statements of clients and citizens' rights and entitlements in conjunction with the Code. I examine the case for this below.

Under the limits of the Code of Ethics the client is not 'protected' when receiving a service from a non-professional, even though the necessity for a Code in these relationships may be equally pressing.

The suggestion can be summarised as follows. If the values and principles in the Code which apply to professional social workers' helping activities are sound independently of professional social work, and cannot plausibly be restricted to that professional activity, then why should they not be extended (in the form of a code of ethics) to other similar (i.e. less clearly professional) types of activity? The beneficial effect of a code of ethics on a wide range of caring may far outweigh the hope of being able to actually regulate the activities of a more restricted group of professional social workers. The hope that the benefits of a restricted definition of social work may 'protect' clients is probably unrealistic if clients are unable to obtain, read or understand their implied entitlements under the Code even though their lawyers may, or if, on any occasion on which they have good reason to suppose that their social worker has contravened, for example, the Principles of Practice paras. 10, 4 and 5, no method of complaint or possible compensation is available to them other than recourse to another social worker, or to no one at all.

Regulating the attitudes of professionals and non-professionals to 'protect' clients is an indirect method of ensuring that the client obtains his/her entitlements. The Code also sets out ways in which this should be done in terms of attitudes, recognising the client's value and dignity. More positive formulations of clients' entitlements can be added to the Code by examining (a) the position of the client as a citizen of a Welfare State, and (b) statements of rights and entitlements made on behalf of, and by, clients.

I am not here arguing that there should not be a code for professional social workers, but that there is a danger that the content of the Code in terms of values will be associated too exclusively with those to whom the Code is addressed. In short, values can be common to workers and client, though qualifications are not.

Clients as citizens

The Code sets out principles which, if they influence professional social work, will provide the clients with a service without any detriment to him or her in terms of stigma, arbitrary or excessive use of discretionary powers, demeaning procedures of unnecessary tests of entitlement. That clients are citizens has been noted elsewhere:

> in a welfare state there should be no status of 'dependent' removing the recipient of state aid from the position of an ordinary citizen, except in so far as it is necessary for the protection of other citizens (as in the case of some mentally subnormal people and some delinquents). It is one important strand

of welfare state ideology that the recipients of welfare services are not in any way excluded from the basic status of citizen with all the rights that pertain thereto. (Campbell 1978, p. 50)

The Code not only addresses the client–social worker relationship, but also the relationships which exist between the client and the state. Certain procedures exist to regulate which *citizens* become *clients* and receive social services, and the Code is equally relevant to these procedures. Clients receive services because they are citizens and not solely because they have become clients. It is possible that designating a citizen as a client, and providing him with services, sometimes gives the state the opportunity to give that citizen as client less than most citizens would accept. For example, patients/clients in psychiatric hospitals often accept living conditions which are quite unlike real life, as if such conditions are intrinsic to treatment. Such conditions in fact are the result of status. This can be seen in terms of privacy, choice of menu, mobility and transport to and from the hospital and access to information, complaints procedures, and in some cases their own funds. Patients or clients may also have a low standard of living, in or out of hospital, which is designated 'care' or 'after-care'. Similarly, employment opportunities for disabled persons are considerably worse than for the general population and yet few of the social services which they receive address this basic entitlement. The trend towards receipt of Invalidity Benefit by ex-psychiatric patients illustrates this further. It is frequently the case that this category of client would be regarded as capable of work under more favourable economic circumstances. The higher benefit in financial terms 'compensates' for the relinquishing of the right to some form of employment. The Code may be usefully considered in this light, recognising that there are certain paradoxes in being a 'client' if 'clienthood' becomes a poor substitute for 'citizenship'. It may even encourage lower expectations and giving up certain claims. In a discussion of client rights as citizen's rights clarification of the word 'right' is required. It is possible to draw a distinction between 'claim rights' (which are enshrined in the form of legislation or statute) and moral rights (which may not clearly specify a duty to fulfil them). However the existence of implied legal or claim rights is a problem in the welfare field. This can be seen in legislation which is passed but not fully implemented or in expressions of legislative intent and White Paper guidelines. For example in the White Paper *Better Services for the Mentally Ill* (HMSO, 1975), citizens and clients are presented with guidelines for service provision which in many parts of the United Kingdom are not met. The claim by a client for community mental health facilities is not formally a legal right but a moral aspiration. Whether it ought to be or not is a further moral question. I suggest later that social worker/client relationships are not limited to transactions of service but may also be collaborative enterprises in search of a goal, in this example for day care facilities.

The notion of clients as fellow citizens has been developed in the BASW publication *Clients are Fellow Citizens* (1980). The emphasis in relation to Mental Health Services here was on the sharing of information; the rules of natural justice in compulsory hospital admissions; the rights of appeal to tribunals; affirmation of the right to neutral second opinions; and crucially that social workers should assume that clients labelled mentally disordered are responsible for their actions unless there is clear behavioural evidence to the contrary. Here is a serious attempt to link the rights of clients within helping relationships with the attitude we commonly take to our own rights as citizens. The quote above notes the relationship between (clients') rights and responsibility. Responsibility is here understood as a capacity, and the 'right' is facilitated by recognition of it by the social worker.

Three categories of client entitlement

I now wish to show that the Code lends itself to a broader attempt to improve services to clients which can be based not on the idea of 'protection' of clients by regulation of a limited number of social workers, but on an examination of the additional sources of statements of rights and entitlements which governments, professionals and clients have drawn up. The Code of Ethics concerns itself with principles which should inform practice. Although it is 'not a manual of practice' a test of its usefulness is to see how principles affect social work action.

Social work services are provided for clients with variation in the degree of co-operation, partnership and direct service with the client and other agencies. These can be briefly described as follows.

1   Those where a direct social worker–client transaction takes place where the substance of the transaction can be controlled and provided by the social worker; for example, counselling, support, information-giving.

2   Those claimed by the client which are the responsibility of a social worker's employers but which do not fall under the control of the individual social worker, and where there may be an absence of regular service; for example, day centre facilities, remedial teaching facilities, a sheltered workshop, or supported hostel accommodation.

3   Those aspects which require the pursuit of client rights and entitlements by the social worker and the client from an additional appropriate source; for example, the service of a disablement resettlement officer, employment rehabilitation courses, housing, social security benefits, medical treatments.

The Code addresses all these situations and the social worker may find in (2) and (3) that his obligations to the client far outweigh his own power to meet the clients needs.

There are three sources of material which may assist both social worker and client to put their case.

1   General declarations of human rights.
2   Statute, legal rights; social and economic policy.
3   Charters, manifestos, and expressions of need by clients themselves.

The Code of Ethics recognises in paragraph 9 of its Principles and in paragraph 10 of the Principles of Practice that the client may have entitlements, needs and rights which cannot be met by the discharge of the direct service provided by the social worker. The Code goes on to state that the social worker has therefore a responsibility to bring to the notice of any 'appropriate source' the needs and claims of the client.

Two common consequences follow from this: first, that the relationship between the social worker and the client becomes focused on an external goal in partnership, and secondly that these external entitlements are pursued by invoking a further specific set of entitlements. It is the second aspect of this process which links the general aspects of the Code of Ethics for the social worker with other positive statements of entitlements for clients.

In pursuing this particular aspect of the Code, reference can be made to a variety of sources. These can be ordered in terms of ability to provide a basis on which the social worker and the client pursue specific goals. I will outline three categories of such statements in relation to the Code which may assist both social workers and clients.

General declarations of human rights

The first category covers those documents which provide broad statements of human rights. The United Nations Declaration of Human Rights in its section on the Rights of Disabled Persons, for example, clearly states a right that disabled people 'are entitled to measures designed to enable them to become as self-reliant as possible', 'according to their capacities to secure and retain employment or to engage in productive and remunerative occupation . . . to participate in social, creative and recreational activities' and '. . . social integration and re-integration'.

The European Convention on Human Rights Article 5 (4) states: 'Everyone who is deprived of his liberty by arrest or detention shall be entitled to take proceedings by which the lawfulness of his detention shall be decided speedily by a court and his release ordered if the detention is not lawful.'

This first category of statements of entitlement for clients illustrates a possible development from the Code to positive statements of client entitlement as contrasted with the regulation of service provided by the social worker. However, two questions emerge from this. First, how can such broad statements of principle be used as the basis for a claim and achieved in practice? These general statements are not distinctively British and also speak of the *form* of services that should be delivered rather than their detailed content. Second, is there a dilemma facing social workers within the terms of paragraph 3 of the Foreword of the Code if the 'obligations to . . . their employers' and their respnsibilities in paragraph 7 of the principles regarding management of the organisation's resources conflict with the practical achievement of the goals for the client? It may be the case that the Local Authority social worker finds himself in conflict with his employer. This may result from the social worker pursuing *with* the client rights – which can, or should, be met by another 'appropriate source' (para.

10) and in doing so discovering that the other source is in fact the Local Authority who employs him.

This problem can be illustrated by describing the way in which statutory services regard themselves as having certain limits to their activity and that responsibilities for clients may be transferred from one service to another. These transfers are real for clients and often well managed by social workers, for example the transition from old people's home to geriatric ward, or from psychiatric hospital to social service day care. However there are occasions when the social worker may not only value continuity of care and management highly, and wish to be involved, but also where in order to provide an effective service the social worker must create change within his own organisation in order that the other appropriate source can play its full part in the process of continuing care. The social worker working as a mental health officer, for example, will be involved in compulsory and voluntary admissions to psychiatric hospital. I show in detail below how in the full discharge of his obligations to the client, the social worker's and client's priorities may conflict with his employer's view of their obligations. These matters, usually at a practical level, become the subject of the second category of statements of entitlements in statute, and the implementation of social policy.

There remains however the question of the usefulness of declarations of human rights in general terms as background to the Code of Ethics. The idea that Britain would benefit from a Bill of Rights, a substantive statement of citizens' rights, has been suggested by Lord Scarman (1974). He suggested that a Bill of Rights should be specific and includes 'first of all, due process, natural justice, rules of procedure and some substantive rights'.

Scarman agreed with Lord Hailsham who noted 'the helplessness of law in the face of the legislative sovereignty of Parliament which makes it difficult for the legal system to accommodate the concept of fundamental and inviolable human rights'. Dahrendorf has suggested that demands for a Bill of Rights are a symptom of the breakdown of consensus and that 'A Bill of Rights that is a set of guarantees of fundamental individual rights which is entrenched and incorporated in law is probably the only way in which the individual can defend himself against the overpowering institutions of modern society'. The Code of Ethics notes that 'social workers are often at the interface between powerful organisations and relatively powerless applicants for service' (Statement of Principles, para. 9). Social workers may regard a British Bill of Rights as a useful reference point in discharging their obligations to clients as informed by the Code of Ethics.

Therefore, to return to the questions posed at the beginning of this section, how can broad statements be used as the basis for a claim, and how is the social worker assisted in resolving agency conflict concerning the scope of personal and organisational obligations?

First, individual claims to European courts have been successful in cases of compulsory detention in psychiatric hospitals without appeal to a court; and in campaigns against corporal punishment in schools. Second, the social worker within his agency and in relation to an 'appropriate source' can refer to an external justification for pursuing client rights when in doing so he may contravene local structural arrangements.

Statute, legal rights, social and economic policy

The second category of statements includes laws and statutes, appeals to the ombudsman and civil proceedings. These are often encountered by clients as regulations regarding, for example, social security, housing, admission to care and other 'social' legislation. These can be invoked for the client by the social worker and are frequently not the direct responsibility of the Local Authority social worker's employer. There are two important aspects of these sources of entitlements. First, that a close knowledge of them by social workers (and a clear interpretation for the client) will increase the extent to which the 'rule of law' can be operative in social service provision and a reduction in the extent to which rights for the client may be 'discretionary'. Second, that the existence of much social welfare legislation conferring general powers on local authorities does not always go hand in hand with a willingness to provide resources for a social policy or to produce actual services for the individual client or citizen. A close analysis of the relationship between statutory obligations of local authorities, the absence of social policy guidelines, and services for clients may result in the client wishing to take action under the law to achieve satisfaction, but finding difficulty in doing so.

An example of the extension of the Code of Ethics (para. 9, Statement of Principle, and para. 10, Principles of Practice) to statements of client entitlements which require the examination of 'other appropriate sources' of help outside the direct regulation of social work practice can be provided in the following case example.

A person who is suffering from a mental illness and who is also regarded by his local doctor as being potentially a danger to himself and others is compulsorily admitted to a psychiatric hospital for twenty-eight days. The next-of-kin is not readily available and the social worker acting as a mental health officer agrees on the need for admission in the absence of any alternative form of care or service.

The social worker at this point may cease involvement with the client, and this *is* frequently the case.[1]

However, the Code of Ethics suggest that there exists for social workers 'a responsibility to help clients to obtain *all* those services and rights to which they are entitled, both from the agency in which he works, and from any other appropriate source' (Principles of Practice, para. 10). In this example this responsibility can only be discharged by considering the following aspects of the case.

(a) If the next-of-kin had been informed would they have objected to compulsory admission, put forward alternative methods of care, including themselves, and/or refused to make the application for admission?

(b) Could the crisis have been averted by a swifter and more knowledgeable response from existing services? Are there any alternative forms of care available; for example, a crisis intervention team?

(c) If the social worker has acted for the next of kin, and also is aware of the right of the patient under the European Convention of Human Rights and the mental health legislation to appeal against detention, should they consider an appeal to the court by the patient; inform the patient and next-of-kin of the patient's right, and obtain legal aid for such an appeal?

(d) What kinds of linkage with the community can be sustained by the patient during a hospital stay? Could a review of income maintenance and other consequences of hospitalisation usefully be made?

(e) An examination of the client's requirements could be made in terms of after-care services and particularly housing and employment. Has the examination been informed by the statutory obligations to provide such services, the existing level of provision and the ability of the social worker to invoke the relevant statements of rights and entitlements due to the client?

These questions raise not only the matter of the extent to which the social worker interprets the scope of his activity (and they thereby support the case for a Code of Ethics which raises such questions) but also takes up an earlier theme of a discrepancy between the social worker's view of client needs and the view of his employers. It does so against the backdrop of a stream of social service legislation which is distinguished for the client usually by social and economic policy rather than by an awareness of a legal right. The client is in a particularly disadvantageous position in respect of a contract with a social worker who acts as an agent of the local authority, which in itself has a general duty, for example, to 'provide social welfare'. The client can neither easily seek redress against an individual social worker because of the nature of this contract nor can he/she insist on an individual interpretation of such words as 'after-care' within the social service legislation. The Code recognises this when it says 'the social workers' responsibility for relief of hardship and suffering is not always fully discharged by direct service to individual families and groups. He has the right and duty to bring to the attention of those in power, and of the general public, ways in which the activities of government, society or agencies, create or contribute to hardship and suffering or militate against their relief.' Social workers using the Code will therefore be encouraged to view not only legislation and statute as a basis for client entitlements but also to consider the effects of social and economic policy at both regional and national level.

Fashions in social policy such as 'community care', 'self-help' or 'voluntary activity' sometimes exploit an ambiguity in their meaning. They may be used in times of scarce resources to shift responsibility for meeting client needs and rights excessively on to individuals, families, or communities and divert attention, on economic grounds, from the relationship of the client as a citizen between him and the state. 'Welfare' masquerading as rights can be more easily regulated than 'fundamental individual rights' which may be inviolably enshrined in a Bill of Rights. The shift of responsibilities from institutions to families under the policy of 'community care' (for the mentally handicapped, mentally ill, or elderly) may not be a provision of a social service to meet client needs so much as a transfer of costs from the 'formal economy' to the 'domestic economy' and a shift of the burden of care on to relatives. The Code in the Statement of Principles states that recognition of the client's value should be irrespective of status. The Code however does not address in detail the question of the client's ability to pay or make use of other sources in kind which surround them and which may be used as part of a programme of care for the client.

We can therefore return to the Code (paras. 7, 8 and 9 in the Statement of Principles), which declares its adherent's concern for 'social planning', 'evaluation of methods and policies' and scrutiny of the 'activities of government' in so far as they impinge upon the 'realisation of [clients'] rights and the satisfaction of his needs', and consider whether these responsibilities have been discharged.

The Code may appear a little fragile in the face of this lack of implementation of social legislation; the absence of a Bill of Rights and the economics of social policy itself increasingly includes the theme of individual responsibility and freedom of choice.

In these circumstances the 'sense of responsibility' and therefore the scope of activity of the social worker will have some relationship to the power that the social worker has to obtain the rights and services that the client requires and to the extent of the discrepancy between the spirit and implementation of social legislation. However, here the Code should make the worker consider whether the needs of the client 'impose obligations which cannot be fulfilled', and therefore the client must adjust to what the social worker judges to be reality, or whether we can act under paragraph 9 of the Statement of Principles and state the client's case. Some way may then be found both for the social worker to discharge his/her obligations in partnership with the client. This is a potential strength of the Code, that it overtly, 'explicitly' (para. 1) shows the ability of social workers to follow through their principles and the client's requirements *at various levels*. This also illustrates, however, the danger of the Code being used as the internal regulating mechanism of a narrow group of professional social workers. Social workers might wrongly consider it ethically sound to exercise authority in relation to the client by presenting, upholding and thereby perpetuating the reality of absence of service, and consider this to be therapeutic in the best interests of the client, and *then separately* pursue their collective professional objections to the absence of resources (under para. 9, Statement of Principles). This activity by social workers separates them from their clients. It runs the risk of being regarded as an attempt to attract resources to the profession as opposed to the client. It also excludes the clients from collectively stating their case (or acquiring the skills to do so). This is not to say that there are not times when social workers must accept and help clients to accept that they will not obtain their entitlements. However, it is worthwhile to consider ways in which this tension can be resolved without the Code of Ethics for professional social workers encouraging the idea that the social work profession can pursue matters of resources and policy on behalf of the client, and encouraging the client to be passive. The third category of statements of rights and entitlements noted below is the basis for the client and worker to be jointly active.

The Code assumes an ability on the part of social workers to distinguish clearly their direct activity in relation to the client from their contribution to social planning, given that the Code cannot be a manual of practice guidance (Commentary on the Code, para. 3). The social worker is expected to function in three ways. First, to ensure the fullest possible realisation of the client's rights and satisfaction of his needs (para. 9, Statement of Principles). Second, to hold himself 'responsible for the standard of service which he gives' (para. 10.7). Third, to contribute to 'social planning and action' (para. 10.10). There is potentially considerable tension beween these responsibilities. The Code provides a clear justification for the social worker who is unable to provide an adequate standard of service to discharge his responsibilities to the client by insisting that the fact be noted in planning processes. These processes commonly take place further up the hierarchy within which the social worker operates. This contribution to planning is not often clearly seen as an intrinsic part of the discharging of the social worker's responsibility to the client. Furthermore, the existence of channels which allow the social worker to contribute to planning may create conditions under which it is morally tolerable for the social worker to hold himself responsible for standards of service. The Code of Ethics recognises therefore that social workers would find it difficult to accept responsibility for services which they are powerless to improve. However, frequently the social worker finds himself in practice in the position outlined in paragraph 8 of the Code, recognising 'that the competence of his particular discipline is limited', and he may also be working in an under-resourced, unfashionable area of social work practice. In these circumstances clear thinking about the ways in which the social worker may fulfil his obligations (to the client) is crucial. The case illustration above is such a situation. The aspect of intervention in (a), (b) and (c) could be expanded to include an extensive checklist of activity properly undertaken by social workers in this situation.[2]

This is not to be dismissed as an ideal model if we are taking the Code seriously, but as an exploration of the possible entitlements of the client.

From the illustration given above it is clear that a full appraisal of the client's rights and the obligations of the social worker on the basis of the Code of Ethics leads to a considerable expansion of activity. This expansion lends itself to a consideration of the conditions under which social work in practice can achieve change. The Commentary on the Code of Ethics itself notes: 'New ideas about social work and changes in its environments will necessitate revision of the Code from time to time' (para. 1). Change can occur within social work practice as a result of the pursuit of clients' entitlements and these may often be pursued on the basis of the third category of such statements.

Charters, manifestos, statements of client needs and rights

These statements have the greatest potential for promoting joint activity between social workers and clients in order to explore new ways to meet needs, bring pressure to bear on the existing system for change, and to act on shared values when the client's needs are not fulfilled. These types are often in the form of constitutions of interest groups, pressure groups or voluntary organisations; this category would also include statements such as the Patient's Charter[3] or MIND: The National Association for Mental Health's Manifesto and principles set out in *Common Concern*, statements of children's rights, goals of self-help groups and the Women's movement.

The relationship between client needs and rights is important here. Clearly not all demands are rights. However, if needs form the basis of rights, the person who is in receipt of benefit would have a moral right to such benefit. A full description of the relationship between 'needs' and 'rights' can be found in R. Plant *et al.*, *Political Philosophy and Social Welfare* (1980, chs. 3 and 4) and in Plant's contribution to Timms (1980). The basic needs to which Plant refers are 'survival' and 'autonomy': the need for survival is to be satisfied by various types of forbearance including forbearing against killing; the need for autonomy by forbearing against interference; but at the same time, they are also to be satisfied by various sorts of resource provision without which the needs recognised negatively by forbearance cannot be satisfied. Clearly which 'needs' can be legitimately claimed as 'rights' is a matter of dispute, and also the levels of satisfaction will be a matter of normative dispute. Statements of needs by clients or endorsed by clients in the various forms mentioned above are important additional sources for social workers in interpreting their obligations within the Code of Ethics in relation to the encouragement of self-realisation of the individual person (Statement of Principles, para. 6). Crudely, social workers will take account of what clients say they want in deciding how to act. The background to this discussion has been well expressed by Feinberg.

> I accept the moral principle that to have unfulfilled need is to have a kind of claim against the world, even if against no-one in particular . . . . Such claims based on need alone, are permanent possibilities of rights, the natural seed from which rights grow. When manifesto writers speak of them as if already actual rights, they are easily forgiven, for this is but a powerful way of expressing the conviction that they ought to be recognised by states here and now as potential rights and consequently as determinants of present aspirators and guides to *present* policies. (1973, p. 67)

This category of statement will influence the social worker's interpretation of his responsibilities under paragraph 9 of the Statement of Principles in the Code of Ethics: 'in view of the applicant's lack of power, social workers have a special responsibility to ensure the *fullest possible* realisation of his rights and satisfaction of his needs' (emphasis added). The practical aspects of what can be realistically regarded as the 'fullest possible' by social workers can be heavily influenced by the statements and the activities noted under the third category of statements of clients' rights and entitlements particularly when voluntary organisations and/or self-help groups illustrate new directions for assistance and service and claim existing rights more actively.

Summary

I began this discussion by noting the difficulties associated with limiting a Code of Ethics to professional social workers. The tenets set out in the Code will clearly find a large measure of support from a much broader group of people involved in caring. I have suggested also that clients themselves are encouraged to share caring values as part of the service they receive, for example in therapeutic communities and self-help groups. The case illustration has shown that social workers' obligations can sometimes be fulfilled in relation to the client only by generalising the client's problem and examining critically the limits imposed on the activities of people like him or her. The third category of sources provides a way in which these two difficulties can be met.

If the tenets of the Code find an echo in the values of volunteers, informal carers and clients themselves, and if social workers are often required to see their obligations as fulfilled by exerting pressure on agencies, and systems, including their own, to improve and increase resources, the social workers' and clients' interests converge. It is therefore amongst the statements of clients' entitlements such as manifestos, charters and voluntary pressure groups that a real practical extension of the obligations in the Code of Ethics can be found. Without reference to the three categories of statements of clients' rights and entitlements a code of ethics may remain a statement by social workers about social work rather than a basis for meeting clients' needs.

The Code of Ethics not only regulates activity and services provided by social workers but also encourages social workers to examine clients' entitlements to services which their employers may provide and services which other agencies may provide. The Code lends itself to an exploration of statements of entitlements in the latter two aspects of social work. A threefold description of such statements is suggested:

    (a)   General declarations of rights; and the place of a Bill of Rights.
    (b)   Statutory and legal rights; and the role of social policy.
    (c)   Charters and manifestos; and the clients' collective expressions of need.

The Code itself encourages social workers to consider all three categories of statements of entitlements and seek thereby to fulfil their obligations under the Code of Ethics.

7 The ethics of residential social work

John R. Hudson

Introduction

Residential social work presents particular difficulties in any consideration of social work ethics not least because there is no consensus about the relationship between social work and residential provision. Since 'the point of any code of ethics . . . depends upon *our conception of the nature of social work*' (Watson, ch. 1 of this book), I would like, before moving on to the main theme, to set out my conception of residential social work.

There was a tendency in England and Wales during the late 1960s to regard residential provision as a particular form of social group work. In the early 1970s the analysis of social services into levels (Rowbottom *et al.*, 1974) was applied to residential provision, appearing most notably in the report of the CCETSW Working Party on Education for Residential Social Work (CCETSW, 1973). According to this analysis social work is one of a number of levels of work within a residential establishment. The Barclay Report (Barclay, 1982) carries on this notion of levels in its analysis of the 'tending' aspect of residential provision. At the same time a number of people (Williams, 1973; Ward, 1977) began to identify residential social work as a specific social work method. More recently, under American influence, the concept of 'group care' (Wolins, 1974) has been developed to include practice settings outside social work, i.e. in the medical, educational and justice networks (Ainsworth and Fulcher, 1981). While I have considerable sympathy with the last position, none has fully satisfied me.

First, I know from my own experience that residential work is not synonymous with groupwork: helping people in a residential setting requires varying combinations of individual, family and groupwork approaches. Second, I am aware that many of the 'skills' of residential social work are common to other forms of residential provision and other forms of social work. I have therefore found it difficult to draw any meaningful boundaries round the concept of 'residential social work' as a social work method. Equally I have found it difficult to allocate any particular 'skill' or piece of work to a level since many of the 'skills' are common to a number of levels and any particular piece of work usually involves more than one 'skill'. Third, whilst I find the concept 'group care' useful in identifying similar approaches to helping people, I find it too general to tease out the specific elements 'social work' and 'residential care' since, by definition, it includes day care.

My own approach for more than a decade has been somewhat different. Taking my cue from a German colleague (Burchhardt, 1971), who argues that 'residential child care' is nothing more than a shorthand for 'child care in a residential setting', I have chosen to view social work and residential provision as in separate conceptual categories. Other members of the category 'profession' – in which I include social work – would be medicine, law and education. Other members of the category 'settings' – in which I include residential provision – would be homes, offices, streets, playgrounds and day centres (including day schools as opposed to boarding schools which are part of residential provision).

It follows from this approach that (1) the expression 'residential social work' must be taken as shorthand for 'social work in a residential setting' and (2) the acknowledged differences between field and residential social work lie *not* in different methods and 'skills' but in the different demands of the respective settings. More recently, I have become dissatisfied with this approach and the conception of residential social work which I shall adopt in discussing the theme of this book draws on developments in systems thinking.

A key concept in systems thinking is 'emergence', the idea that systems have certain properties which are properties of a system but not of any of its subsystems. These properties are called the 'emergent properties' of the system. To give a simple illustration, full descriptions of H_2 and O do not together fully describe water. In systems terms, the 'emergent properties' of water are those which are not comprised in the separate descriptions of H_2 and O. Checkland (1981) points out that this concept has a long pedigree stretching back to the Aristotelian maxim: 'the whole is greater than the sum of its parts.'

I shall therefore base the remainder of what I have to say on my conceptions of social work and residential provision as having characteristics which distinguish them respectively from other 'professions' and 'settings' and of residential social work as a system having 'emergent properties' which cannot be located anywhere in descriptions of either social work or residential provision. It seems to me that this conception has the further merit of 'accounting for' several approaches to residential social work. The notion of levels can be seen to arise from the observation of the properties of residential provision and the emergent properties of residential social work. The idea of residential social work as a social work method can be seen as an attempt to describe the emergent properties of residential social work without the necessary conceptual tools. Burchhardt's approach of drawing attention to the separate elements helps to identify relevant subsystems in the system 'residential social work'. A drawback is the lack of agreement about conceptions of social work and the creation of a system with such a nebulous subsystem may be regarded by some as singularly speculative. So be it. I shall look first at some features of the ethics of residential social work in relation to other chapters in this book and then move on to aspects which may be peculiar to residential social work.

In whose interests?

Payne (ch. 5, this volume) draws attention to problems in identifying a client's best interests and in balancing the needs of the individual with the needs of the wider group. This is a particular problem in residential social work both because of the nature of residential provision and because of the encouragement of more permeable residential units. Permeability is the extent to which those inside and those outside can cross the boundary of the institution. Residential provision can vary from the virtually impermeable (or 'closed institution') through varying degrees of the permeability, e.g. staff are free to come and go but residents are not, to the highly permeable where staff, residents and visitors are free to come and go throughout much of the day and night.

Since residential provision involves dealing with individuals within and through a larger group, any professional judgment or action has an impact on both the individual and the group. This is a characteristic of most forms of group care and a frequent topic of discussion among those who work in group care. But the impact of a residential social worker's judgments or actions may spread to those who are *not* clients or those whose status as a client is unclear.

For example, where one of the aims of admitting someone to residential care is to meet the needs of the family, a number of possible relationships may develop between the residential social worker and family. They may be treated as members of the wider community, as co-therapists, as clients or, very often, as clients of the agency but not of the residential social worker. Equally, since all relationships involve some degree of mutuality, they may relate to the residential social worker in a number of different ways. Whatever the nature of the residential social worker's relationships with the family, they will have some impact on the extent to which the resident's needs can be met.

Some residential provision involves dealing with members of society who are not formally clients. The development of 'resource centres' and the support given in the Barclay Report for the idea of residential centres as 'focal points of community-orientated social work' (Barclay, 1982; Berridge, 1982) have highlighted the potential relations any residential provision can have to the wider society. In such homes it is not unusual to find that visitors outnumber residents at certain times of the day and that among those visitors are some who have needs that can be met within the residential provision. The role of the home may be formally acknowledged by the agency without the relationships with members of the community who use its facilities being consciously defined by anyone. Thus, for example, a mother may visit her child in a children's home or a prospective foster-parent visit a prospective foster-child. Both may be involved in caring activities within the home in preparation for the child's discharge from the children's home. Are these mothers colleagues or clients? What difference does it make? Are there any specific obligations which a residential social worker carries in his relationships with members of the wider society or those whose status is unclear?

As it stands the BASW Code of Ethics identifies obligations to 'clients' and 'society' (para. 3), having defined the 'primary objectives' as making 'implicit principles explicit for the protection of clients' (para. 1). Should the Code be extended to give it more relevance to the more permeable residential units? I shall return to this below in my discussion of confidentiality.

The potentially conflicting obligations a residential social worker has to the people listed in the Code of Ethics (Foreword, para. 3) can be well illustrated by my former position as an officer-in-charge of a home for 16–18-year-olds. To whom did I have obligations? To the clients who were admitted to the home; to those who were *not* admitted because there weren't places or they didn't fit the criteria; to my local management for whom the home offered a local service; to the county council as a whole because it was a county resource; to fieldworkers with unplaceable children; to residential workers with difficult children; to our neighbours not to bring in a hoard of delinquents; to the ratepayers?

While acknowledging with Payne (ch. 5) the power inherent in organisations, I am not pessimistic about the possibilities of influencing organisations by the development of policies and procedures based on good social work practice. When opening the home I referred to above I negotiated an admission procedure that would ensure full professional consideration of each young person to be admitted. Through a system of reviews I also tried to spell out for resident, family, fieldworker and residential worker the obligations each had to the others. It seems to me that such explicit arrangements are useful not only in providing a framework for practice and clarifying the mutual obligations of those involved in a home but also for opening up the debate as to whether the precise expression of these mutual obligations is in the best interests of all those who might be involved.

So, in spite of arguing that there are particular difficulties for the residential social worker in identifying who is the client and whether residential social workers have specific obligations to the wider society, I still believe there are two ways forward which are not mutually exclusive. One is to be more explicit in organisational terms about professional responsibilities; the other is to build on recognition of clients as citizens. The development of more permeable institutions as 'focal points of community-orientated social work' (Barclay, 1982) would seem to demand this since the distinction between citizens who are clients and those who are not breaks down in such institutions.

Prejudice

Related to the question 'in whose interests?' is the problem of differential treatment by residential workers, and I would like to draw attention to two types of difficulty.

The first is the temptation to evaluate behaviour in terms of acceptance of the institution and dependence on it and the tendency to suppress that 'deviant' behaviour which creates risks or appears to imply ambivalent feelings about the institution. Thus an elderly gentleman who takes walks from an old people's home in search of his recently deceased wife or to return to familiar haunts may be drugged or supervised to stop him 'being a nuisance' and help him get used to his new surroundings. The conformist's behaviour is evaluated positively; the non-conformist is judged to be in need of drugs or supervision ostensibly to protect himself or society.

The second is the temptation to make judgments which favour residents rather than other members of society. Residents may be protected from relatives alleged or known to have been cruel; services may be demanded for them beyond those available to others; facilities may be available to them that are unavailable in the wider society. Positive discrimination may be justifiable; it may be necessary for self-realisation. But it may also develop, as may certain types of restrictive behaviour, from the residential worker's feelings about certain types of behaviour, e.g. granny battering or incest, to which the resident may have been subjected by the family.

In drawing attention earlier to the problems of clarifying in whose interest a residential social worker should act, I omitted to mention the traditional way of regulating field and residential workers' responsibilities – namely, that the fieldworker is responsible for the family and the residential worker for the resident. The 'keyworker concept' (BASW/RCA, 1976) was an attempt to bring greater flexibility to the sharing of these responsibilities but so far little progress appears to have been made.

One reason may be that the traditional pattern allows residential social workers to continue to base their judgments on the best interests of the individual resident without considering the needs of the family. Any movement from this pattern involves abandoning a traditional bias in favour of the resident and accepting ambivalent feelings about both the family and the resident. Since ambivalent feelings are painful and get in the way of clear-cut judgments, there may be pay-offs in retaining the traditional pattern.

Confidentiality

Establishments vary widely in their handling of written and unwritten material. Variations include, for example: (1) all conversations between residents and staff are the property of the whole caring team; (2) conversations between residents and staff may be divulged to senior staff; (3) staff may decide what they divulge. Methods of recording also vary: some homes like to keep files which are open to all other professionals and managerial staff; some keep logs which are selectively transferred to files; a few keep logs which are strictly confidential to the staff of the home and a separate set of files which are open to outside professionals.

I have always taken the view that staff should (1) not be compelled to divulge confidences; (2) have access to senior staff to discuss confidential material with a guarantee that it would not go further without the resident's permission. *So far* I have never received or known anyone else to receive a confidence so vital as to make such an approach invalid on higher principles (e.g. serious risk to others) but that may reflect my particular experiences. The problems I have had have led me to conclude that the vast majority of problems of confidentiality do not occur at the serious end but rather in the middle ground.

For example, a person confides to the fieldworker and then expects that the fieldworker will or will not pass on that confidence; either they address the residential worker in terms that imply they expected the residential worker to be aware of the information or the residential worker alludes to it when they had regarded it as confidential between themselves and the fieldworker. In the first instance the residential worker blames the fieldworker for being unprofessional; in the second the resident blames the fieldworker for being unprofessional. The whole scenario can also be played the other way round.

Similarly residential workers may not always be explicit to residents about those with whom they will share confidences and the resident may receive feedback in an unexpected way thereby creating mistrust between himself and the staff. Some residential workers make explicit the way they will handle information both among themselves and among residents and this can prevent problems but may also raise other questions.

First, it is not always possible to be explicit since the professional relationship between a residential social worker and a member of society may be unclear. If a residential social worker working in a highly permeable residential unit learns that a particular girl has gonorrhoea but has not told her sexual partner, is the social worker's responsibility to the girl or to the partner? Does it make a difference if the girl is a client and the partner not? Or vice versa? If both are clients? Or neither? If the information was received as a confidence or accidentally? Should a residential social worker's code, particularly for those working in highly permeable institutions, include an explicit principle of confidentiality which goes further than simply 'the protection of clients'?

Second, if the first question can be answered and there are explicit arrangements about the handling of confidences so that only selected material will be communicated to other professionals, will this raise questions in others' minds as to the willingness of the staff to collaborate with other professionals and ultimately hinder the work of the home? Or will it encourage greater trust between social workers and members of society and so further the development of social work?

If residential social work is to develop in more permeable institutions, social work ethics need to take into account professional behaviour towards those who are neither clients nor colleagues. I shall return to this later.

Personal and professional values

I referred earlier to the admissions procedure established at the home of which I was officer-in-charge. When I was involved in discussing with fieldworkers prospective residents for the home, I noticed that the fieldworkers who made the most convincing cases for admission and collaborated most effectively with staff were those with a clear commitment to their clients which seemed to go beyond a professional interest. I have also noted that where I have felt more personally committed to a resident it has induced me to undertake the professional aspects of my work more thoroughly. I mention this because I tried at one stage deliberately to separate my personal and professional life but found it impracticable. Particularly when I wanted very much to enable a resident to achieve some change in his or her behaviour I found myself becoming more personally involved. This experience may be supported by the findings of social learning research that change is more likely to occur where there is a nurturing relationship between model/ reinforcer and subject (Lamb, 1981). Jordan (1979), describing his own experiences, argues that a social worker can only act convincingly out of personal conviction, and Payne (ch. 5; cases 7, 8 and 9) illustrates that attempting to distinguish, for bureaucratic purposes, one's public and one's private role is at least difficult.

A further example may help to illustrate some of the problems of trying to tease out personal and professional relationships in a residential home. A young lady engaged to a young man is known to regularly entertain him overnight in her room in the residential home. One day she approaches a member of staff to ask if she will help them make love as both of them are physically handicapped to the extent that they cannot make love without assistance. This request implies the sort of intimate relationship which cannot be entered into unless there is an overlapping of personal and professional values. This overlap is a necessary part of any attempt to create or recreate a pattern of 'normal' relationships for people whose existing pattern has been suspended or broken down.

The word 'normal' begs the question. For staff in residential homes vary in the level of the relationships they offer to residents. There are those who neither offer nor expect any deep emotional involvement with residents, while there are those who value commitment and intimacy, creating an environment in which the deepest feelings of both love and hate can be expressed without any fear of rejection. Residents in residential homes also vary in the level of the relationships they seek. Davis (1981) has pointed up the relationship between the aims of residential placements and family roles. Thus a resident placed in care as a supplement to family provision may only seek those relationships which supplement an existing pattern of relationships, whereas a resident placed in care as a substitute for family provision may seek the whole range of family relationships including the most intimate in a residential home.

Values at work

The importance of having an ideology, firmly rooted in a value system, for each residential establishment has been stressed by Wolins (1974); choice of value systems appears to be immaterial (Hudson, 1981c) but staff commitment to the ideology is essential (Hudson, 1981d). If successful residential work depends on the values of the workers, a code of ethics for residential social workers has to be more than making 'implicit principles explicit for the protection of clients' (para. 1). Its primary purpose must be to make explicit for the residential social worker those principles which must underlie the ideology of each home.

Observation of all the different forms of residential provision appears to support the idea that choice of value system is relevant only in relation to definition of success. For example, to use Davis's analysis again, a home which aimed to offer family-supplemental care would need to adopt a value system which was compatible with notions of shared care and/or care networks crossing the boundary between the home and the community. A home which aimed to offer family-substitute care would need to adopt a value system compatible with long-term commitment and the development of intimate relationships. But, within that limitation, whether the value system was conservative or liberal, marxist or anarchist, Christian or humanist would have no effect on the success of the home.

What does affect the success of the home is a staff team uncommitted to or divided over an ideology. This has a number of consequences for the residential social worker. First, there is no point in continuing to work in a staff team whose ideology conflicts with one's own values. Second, there is no 'right' ideology; within the broad principles of residential social work a very wide range of ideologies are possible. It is better to seek one more in tune with one's own values. Third, there is no point in attempting to undermine an ideology with which one is out of sympathy. This is unlikely to succeed and may ultimately cause more harm than good to the residents (Hudson, 1981b). Two consequences for all social workers are that (1) they must accept a wide range of possible ideologies in their dealings with residential homes, and (2) value systems which may be repugnant to them are just as likely to be successful as ones they are in sympathy with, given the definition of 'success' implied in those value systems.

Families . . .

The involvement of families of residents has been identified as a factor in successful residential care (Walton, 1978; Hudson, 1981a). Indeed, it may be more important for success in residential care than co-operation between field and residential social workers though attention has mostly been focused on this in recent years. As I interpret the evidence to date, successful rehabilitation from residential care is strongly associated with continued family involvement *throughout* the period of residential care. However, successful residential care can also be achieved where there is a conscious decision to break all links with the family and to offer complete family-substitute care. Problems appear to arise where (1) there is an intention to rehabilitate a person from residential care without involving the family throughout the period in residential care, or (2) there is no intention to rehabilitate the person to their family and no provision of an alternative family (which may be a residential home or community or a foster or adoptive home).

One of the problems about family involvement *throughout* a period of residential care is that very often families are resistant to involvement or, where a person has been 'rescued' from a bad family, the professionals wish to restrict involvement. The crucial time appears to be around the admission of the resident when the family's sense of failure is greatest (Hudson, 1975) and can erupt into hostility towards field and residential social workers. As an officer-in-charge I found that parents who visited before or at the time of admission always came again; those who did not never paid a visit.

I raise this issue because the Code of Ethics mentions 'clients' and 'co-operation between those who share professional responsibility' (para. 6) but appears to ignore those whose contribution to social work objectives may be vital but who are not themselves professionals. I have mentioned the development of residential social work that involves working with people who are not clients or whose status is unclear and the need for the Code of Ethics to take into account professional behaviour towards those who are neither clients nor professional colleagues. Since families appear to be so important to successful residential care, perhaps the Code should pay particular attention to the professional behaviour of social workers towards families and others who are collaborators in the social work process. (The contribution of domestic and manual workers also springs to mind here.)

. . . and other professionals

It has always surprised me that (1) I received applications for places from social workers who had made no attempt to evaluate the quality of the placement before asking for the place, and (2) social workers apparently accepted allocation systems for places in residential homes that allowed no evaluation of the merits of the placement for their client. There is always a tension for me in considering any placement particularly as so few residential staff have had the opportunity to undertake professional training and it does seem to me to place two important obligations on professionals: first, to evaluate the staff who are going to care for any resident before agreeing to support a new placement, and second, to offer maximum support to colleagues who have not had the opportunity for professional training.

An essential principle for residential social work?

I have previously suggested (Hudson, 1975) that: *no one should be admitted to residential care unless it can be shown that they will benefit from the admission.* It has been suggested in discussion that this could be restated as a 'do no harm' principle, i.e. that the use of residential care should 'do no harm'.

I prefer my first statement of the principle because it calls for a positive approach. In the first place, it is probably impossible to avoid all types of harm to people even when the outcome may also be very beneficial. Concentrating on avoiding harm may lead to the avoidance of risks and, as with much defensive medicine, a less satisfactory final state. In the second place, many people in residential · care are only seen as needing physical care and not 'social work help'. The danger is that people fail to recognise that human beings need more than just a favourable physical environment to continue living. I suspect that too many people apply mechanical metaphors, such as keeping a clock ticking, to people when such metaphors are too simplistic to apply to simple organisms let alone people.

Residential provision occurs in many forms – schools, hospitals, prisons, convents, barracks, etc. One principle which can distinguish residential social work from mere *provision* is that residents will benefit from the admission. This principle alone is insufficient to distinguish residential social work from, for example, many hospitals and schools but it does distinguish residential social work from 'warehousing' or 'cold storage'.

Conclusion

I have suggested that residential social work is more than just the practice of social work in a residential setting. I have shown that many of the ethical problems that face social workers generally are part of the daily experiences of residential social workers. I have identified two groups in respect of which the obligations of residential social workers might usefully be spelled out further – namely, members of society and families coming into the residential setting – and I have concluded by suggesting a principle which helps to distinguish residential social work from other forms of residential provision in a social welfare system.

8   A doctor looks at A Code of Ethics for Social Work

Joan K. Sutherland

Introduction

I do not propose, in this chapter, to deal with profound matters of moral and ethical standards, their establishment, the motivaton behind this and their acceptance. Rather I shall try to touch in a pragmatic way on the place of a professional ethical code accepted over a considerable period of time by a profession of long standing. I shall try to cover the matters involved, the means by which widespread consensus is reached and how the views of the profession relate to those outside the profession in society at large. Sanctions evolved by the profession and by society at large to prevent gross failure to observe ethical standards will also be identified. Further, I will look at some inconsistencies between various stated principles which arise, and the implications for co-operation between the medical and social work professions.

A personal code or a professional code?

The opinion has been expressed that personal standards of moral and ethical behaviour should extend to an individual's work situation and that there is no need for a separate explicit code in that setting. However, if one is looking at this subject from the point of view of a collective group of workers making up a profession, and that of its patients (or clients), one can see that a member's personal standards extended to his professional conduct intimately involve his colleagues and patients whatever his private standards may be, and that they have a legitimate interest in the explicit expression of those standards because they have a legitimate interest in an explicit set of standards which is mutually acceptable.

What is a profession?

At this point we must try to clarify our conception of a profession. I offer one possible tentative definition: 'a group of persons who have acquired special knowledge and expertise based on a core of knowledge and experience built up over a variable period of time by succeeding generations of participants who have added contributions from research, teaching and experience: a group offering the benefits of its knowledge and skills to the public, usually for financial reward but possibly not'.

The Code begins with the statement, 'social work is a professional activity. Implicit in its practice are ethical principles which prescribe the professional responsibility of the social worker', and goes on to stress that 'social work has developed methods of practice which rely on a growing body of systematic knowledge and experience' (Statement of Principles, para. 7).

As David Watson reminds us, the Barclay Report (1982) discusses the conception of professional social work in detail, pointing out that within the wide spectrum of tasks performed by paid social workers a very great variety of activities is apparent. It is argued that it is necessary to define a narrower group of tasks to be 'professional social work', identified as requiring possession of certain skills and knowledge, including skills in human relationships, and analysis.

Here at least are three views of professionalism which have many common ideas, but in connection with the latter, I might comment that if social workers are employed to perform a series of tasks *some only* of which involve professional social work, this may well give rise to complications for such a worker who will be bound by a professional code in *part* only of his activities and not in others. Likewise he may be accorded the privileges of the professional only in *some* of his duties and not in others.

Does a profession need a code?

In Britain in 1858 at the instigation of the British Medical

Association (speaking as the mouthpiece of the profession) the General Medical Council was established by the Government under the Medical Act. The principle of the Act was expressed in the words: 'It is expedient that persons requiring medical aid should be able to distinguish qualified from unqualified practitioners.' It did not prohibit unqualified practitioners in medicine but any person falsely representing himself as a qualified practitioner could be fined. A register was established and is kept up to date by the General Medical Council (hereafter GMC), and a practitioner convicted of felony or misdemeanour could have his name erased from the register, as could any who 'shall, after enquiry, be judged by the GMC to be guilty of infamous conduct in any professional aspect'.

The conviction that there is a true need for such regulation springs from the real power invested in a group of persons claiming socially useful expert knowledge and skills and the great vulnerability of members of society who invoke their aid. This relationship involves a high degree of trust and for it to function with any success such trust must be shown to be merited.

It must be seen on the one hand that the members of the profession have indeed had the training claimed and, on the other, that they use their knowledge and skills so gained with responsibility and integrity.

What form does a code of ethics take?

Many groups of doctors have developed codes of ethical behaviour applicable to the practice of medicine: these include the International Code of Medical Ethics established by the Declaration of Geneva, amended to its present form at the World Medical Association Assembly in 1968; the Commonwealth Medical Association approved an Ethical Code in January 1984; the Canadian Medical Association has produced a set of Seven Principles of Ethical Behaviour with a guide for their implications for the behaviour of doctors in relationship to the responsibilities to patients, the profession and society; and the Standing Committee of Doctors of the European Economic Community has adopted a Declaration concerning the practice of medicine in the Community which embodies the main ethical principles and their application.

These and other Codes vary in presentation but identify much the same principles: personal interests must not take precedence over those of the patient; professional skills must not be used for inhuman purposes; no bias must be shown in regard to race, creed, social standing or party political stance; medical standards must be maintained and education continued so that advances in knowledge are added to the doctor's expertise; the first loyalty is to the patient, and information given in the course of medical care should not be used for any other purpose without the patient's consent; the possible need for co-operation with other doctors or members of other professions must be recognised and appropriate action in the patient's interest taken.

As David Watson has pointed out in chapter 1, many such principles are not centrally about the work of any particular profession, but here are simply made explicit for members of the medical profession. This fits with the pattern of a basic statement of ethical standards being couched in general terms which may then be extrapolated in a supporting document appropriate to particular situations arising. Such a document will be able to take account of circumstances which may arise from time to time where there is a real dilemma in applying the basic principles, as conditions and attitudes evolve in society.

Do doctors observe the code?

The check on the observance of such a code by the medical profession lies in the hands of the GMC mentioned above. This body is set up by the Government and its composition carefully planned to represent (1) the academic point of view with members from the Medical Schools (to look to the obligation of the Council in relation to proper training having been completed by doctors applying to have their names on the register), (2) the profession of medicine at large with democratic election of medically qualified members from various disciplines within medicine, and geographical areas, and (3) lay members to represent the views of the general public. The Council has highly qualified legal advisers. It has developed a system with which to investigate complaints against the behaviour of any registered medical practitioner.

There is no set of strict rules which must be accepted by a doctor on qualification or registration with punishment inevitable and predictable if one is broken. The general term 'guilty of serious professional misconduct' (words which replaced the original guilty of infamous conduct in any professional aspect in a modification of the Medical Act in 1978) remains to be set alongside any misdemeanour reported to the GMC which then decides whether, if proved, the action amounts to serious professional misconduct, and what punishment to impose: the removal of the culprit's name from the register for a temporary period or indefinitely. The procedures used have been widely discussed within the profession and approved by the representative medical organisations and by the Privy Council.

This looks tidy and secure, but many deviations from perfect, or even desirable, professional behaviour occur. What may be regarded as weakness is that a complaint has to be made initially for action to take place. The natural source of such a complaint would seem to be the party who has suffered as a result of the behaviour in question. Equally, a third party who becomes aware of matters which could merit complaint but have not involved him personally is reluctant to be seen to be the 'reporter'. From experience in recent years it is possible that this attitude may be being reconsidered.

On reflection, the alternative is some higher authority with supervisory power and this directly contradicts the professional autonomy seen by many to be integral to the professional person who undertakes final responsibility for his own professional decisions and actions.

I have been describing the way in which a profession that recognises its power and the vulnerability of its patients has tried to set standards and promote trust in the profession as a whole. All members of the profession may not adhere to these standards any more than all members of a community will keep all laws established by common agreement of that community or all members of a religious group behave always in the way that the group as a whole believes to be right.

How do doctors know about the Code?

The information is called *Professional Conduct and Discipline:*

Fitness to Practice, published by the GMC and circulated to all registered medical practitioners. A section mentions 'certain kinds of professional misconduct and criminal offences which have, in the past, led to disciplinary proceedings or which in the opinion of the Council could give rise to a charge of serious professional misconduct . . . Doctors who seek detailed advice in particular circumstances should consult a Medical Defence Society or Professional Association. The Council can rarely give such advice because of its judicial function' (Part II, paras. 1 and 2).

Where does a professional association fit in?

Here it is that the professional association enters the scene. The British Medical Association (hereafter BMA) amongst other things aims 'to uphold the honour of the profession'. It has had a standing Central Ethical Committee for many years and this Committee is charged with study and elucidation of problems arising in the field of medical ethics. Much of the material springs from policy agreed by members of the Association after debate at the Annual Representative Meeting. The Committee has put together a *Handbook of Medical Ethics* which is offered as a guide in this field to members of the BMA and any others interested. This document and any other recommendations of the Committee are reported to the Council of the Association and, if involving any change in policy, are put before an Annual Representative Meeting of the BMA for modification and adoption, or rejection. The BMA, which has, of course, a voluntary membership and is not a closed shop, has little in the way of sanctions, the ultimate one being expulsion of the member after due enquiry, and they would not claim that this is a severe punishment! But because it is not acting as the judicial body, the Association can, through its Central Ethical Committee, raise discussion on many more detailed ethical problems and express views in more controversial fields than it is possible for the GMC to do.

I would agree with David Watson (ch. 1) about the possibilities of confusion between professional and a professional association and, as will be seen from the above description, the doctors' professional association sees its function in this field as providing a forum for members of the profession, first, to debate more controversial elements of a code of behaviour in an attempt to establish a consensus of opinion, taking account of constantly changing medical techniques and capabilities, and evolving professional and public opinion, and second, to advise its members.

Where does society at large come in?

One must always remember that the legal system also functions in this field and 'malpractice' is not a rare lawsuit. In this case the law undertakes a 'non-medical' investigation taking all necessary evidence into account (including that of an expert medical witness if needed) before making a legal decision and invoking civil or criminal penalties.

It is perhaps worth noting here that in spite of a widespread opinion that doctors 'can get off with anything' and are subject to very little control, they are in fact liable to punitive action in a number of ways for one misdeed: first, they can be found in breach of contract and lose their job if it is in a hospital, or in general practice be subject to financial penalties, or termination of contract; second, they can be temporarily or permanently removed from the Medical Register by the GMC, making employment very difficult to find; or third, they can be sued in the Law Courts!

Are there no inconsistencies?

I now turn to apparent clashes between certain principles. The practice of a profession often provides situations where conflict is seen to arise and priorities have to be decided or compromise attempted. For example, when loyalty to the patient may be at variance with the interests of society at large. The social work profession also faces this clash in their Statement of Principles when they say, 'the profession accepts responsibility to encourage and facilitate the self-realisation of the individual person with due regard for the interests of others' (Statement of Principles, para. 6). The medical profession is perhaps a little more committed to the interests of the patient (placing the regard it does on the patient's ability to trust the doctor), but we all know that very occasionally, unless a doctor is willing to divulge information coming to him in the course of medical care, a serious wrong or grossly traumatic event may take place unless that information is used to avert it. Sometimes this is taken care of by the law, e.g. severe, dangerous and contagious disease is notified by law, so that the community can be protected from epidemic spread of serious illness by an irresponsible individual. A violently deranged mentally ill person can be detained by law to protect him or other members of society. (The professional worker must, of course, comply with the statutory law of the land in which he is working even if it seems to transgress the ethical obligation to the patients unless he feels so strongly that he is prepared to accept legal consequences of his action.) There are, however, situations which arise and are not covered by statute, e.g. where a patient may persist in fulfilling a job in which the public are endangered by a medical condition known to the doctor but kept secret by the patient. There is a range of views within the medical profession on this dilemma but there is general agreement that action by the doctor which appears to promote the interests of others above those of the patient who has consulted him must only be taken in the very extreme case; and only after all means of rational persuasion have been tried and failed. It should be remembered that, leaving aside high ethical principles, if such actions on the part of doctors are anticipated by patients the consultation will probably not be made, and the dangerous situation hidden from doctors and public alike, with, perhaps, worse consequences.

Another dilemma of competing loyalties arises in identifying the duty to the employer and the duty to the patient. This, I feel, is a much more likely occurrence in the social work sphere where many more working situations involve the employer/employee relationship.

This whole area leads us into a very complicated field of discussion. The medical profession was very apprehensive about implications here when arrangements changed in this country from independent provision of medical services, with certain insurance arrangements, to that of a National Health Service provided by the state. Careful thought was given to legal wording of the Acts involved and work contracts. The recent legal procedures connected with the City of Birmingham Authority and access to social work records give much food for thought. One leading member of the legal profession opined as follows:

It is no part of the National Health Service to treat patients. Its function is to provide doctors who will do so. The resulting relationships are (a) employer and employed doctor, (b) doctor and patient. By contrast it is the duty of the Local Authority to care for children and to play a part in their adoption. For this purpose the Local Authority employs social workers. The resulting relationships are (a) Local Authority and employed social worker (b) Local Authority, Social Worker and clients for both. Once this is understood it disposes of the professional objection to revealing confidential information to the members of the local authority on the basis that to do so would be a breach of a professional relationship since this exists not only between the social worker and client, but also embraces the Local Authority itself . . . . Bearing in mind that it is the Local Authority and not the individual social worker which is performing the statutory duty . . . the Social Worker is, as it were, the instrument used by the authority . . . . Confidential information given to the social worker is given to the Authority. However, those who give it are entitled to expect, and the social worker can reasonably assure them that, save as may be necessary for the performance of the local authority's statutory duties, the information will never be divulged to anyone outside the Authority or to anyone within the Authority who has no need to know. (O'N and O'N v. City of Birmingham District Council, Queen's Bench Divisional Court, 19 February 1982)

This, to me, very disturbing assessment is closely linked with the fact that the social work tasks of paid social workers are not all *professional* social work. It is true that in the medical world certain employment situations produce slightly difficult relationships, e.g. a doctor employed by an insurance company providing a medical report on one of his patients with a view to the company arranging insurance for him may appear to act against the interests of the patient in divulging certain medical facts which will make insurance more difficult or costly. Here, however, the patient clearly understands the function that doctor is performing and gives written consent knowing that this is a necessary condition for the purpose he wishes to pursue. Other employer/doctor situations occur but the ethical duty of the doctor is always to ensure that the patient is aware of the position and agrees to it before proceeding.

The problem for the social worker who is employed by a Local Authority and finds himself doubtful about his ability to conform to his professional code appears to be much more complex and to depend on wording of Acts of Parliament, contracts of employment, and identification of tasks falling within the professional social work definition and those outwith it. I find it difficult to accept that an umbrella ethical code (e.g. of confidentiality) extends over the whole membership of a Local Authority who, as far as I am aware, have no explicit code of ethics and no form of sanctions.

Are there any omissions?

In an ever-changing society experiencing rapid advances in scientific knowledge and skills and constantly evolving social and moral attitudes, it would be well nigh impossible to lay down a code of ethics covering all possible situations. Thus, main principles are formulated and individual application has to be made in individual sets of circumstances with constant re-interpretation of the principle concerned.

Some areas are on the fringe of a professional code and it may be that doctors appear irresponsible in this kind of area. Planning and use of resources is one such sphere. It is true that professionals have an ethical obligation to be responsible in the use of resources provided by others which may also be in short supply and expensive, but this kind of responsibility is a general one and not related to a particular profession with a particular knowledge and skill and therefore is not identified in a code of ethics of *one* profession. The doctor is ethically obliged to make available his medical skill and knowledge in advising on resource distribution, but is not professionally responsible for the management planning which ensues therafter (but consider Klein, 1978; McLachlan and McKeon, 1971; and Illich, 1975).

The professional code of ethics relates to uses of professional skills in a privileged professional situation. A general standard of responsible behaviour is expected from the professional person in that one does not expect him to steal from, defraud or physically abuse his patients. Such actions would be a transgression of society's code of behaviour and liable to legal sanctions as such.

Incidentally, of course such behaviour *would* be classified as behaviour likely to bring discredit on the profession and in that way lead to sanctions within the profession as well as outwith it.

There are, no doubt, other instances of 'gaps' in the stated code which will come to light as the milieu in which medicine is practised evolves, and the medical profession is constantly studying such matters – as at present is the case with 'in vitro' fertilisation.

How far is a professional independent in action?

This leads us into the area of professional discretion. BASW states in the Code of Ethics: 'In order to carry out these obligations, the professional has complementary rights which must be respected for him to work effectively (Foreword, para. 4).

The freedom to use professional discretion without any 'higher' lay supervision or authority is one considered by a variety of ethical codes to be of real significance and, indeed, to be one of the distinguishing features of a professional. It does, of course, relate entirely to actions in the field of expertise of the person involved. In the medical scene it is frequently equated with clinical freedom. It is the professional care of patients which is concerned and sometimes the use of resources may impinge on this area. The doctor's proper function here is to advise the managers and those responsible for provision of health services on the need for certain resources. The final decisions are in the hands of the managers and the representatives of the public charged with health care provision. If a doctor feels that, in spite of adequate opportunity to advise, the resources available prevent him from giving responsible care to patients he must inform the patients and the managers of this situation and in the extreme he may feel it necessary to resign from a service where he is unable to fulfil his professional obligations. Of course in a monopoly situation this is a position of extreme difficulty.

In the realm of planning and use of resources I believe the practising professional's function is that of advice and if he feels compelled to make stronger protests about management and resources involving, for example, political action this should be a personal responsibility performed outwith his professional activities and clearly indicated to be so.

Is there any interdependence of professions and their codes?

The understood guidance in the medical world is that a registered member of the medical profession should not co-operate in the care of a patient with an unqualified person (i.e. a person whose knowledge and experience, and ethical professional standards are not established). This does not exclude accepting help in patient care from such people in certain situations if it is in the patient's interests, but the doctor is personally responsible for the outcome of the 'unqualified' person's participation. Integrated sharing of patient/client care develops best when both 'carers' are professionally established and recognise each other's professional integrity and acknowledge similar codes of ethical behaviour with meaningful sanctions. The relationship between the medical and nursing professions is a good example. The professions allied to medicine have now a National Regulatory Body and a Register and the consequential sanctions, so here joint professional care is also safely based.

It is this much more narrow reliance on knowledge and experience which leads the 'traditional' medical profession into what is sometimes seen as a negative or arrogant attitude to what is becoming known as 'alternative medicine' and other methods of handling disease. The traditional medical profession reserves judgment on alternative medicine methods as outwith its field of real knowledge and experience and relies rather on what it sees as well established and proven by its own form of estimation. There is now, however, quite a strong move developing to try to learn more of alternative medical methods in an effort to establish whether some, at least, meet the criteria of traditional medicine.

The modern evolution of 'team work' involving health and social services has given rise to some anxiety. One very obvious example is the conference concerning non-accidental injury of children. In some cases, for instance, the police may have a contribution to make but it has become clear that in the view of many members of the police force the prime importance of the interests of the patient/client and the undertaking to use information only for the purpose for which it was given do not bind them and, indeed, may contravene their proper duty. Thus, information given by a patient to a doctor for the purpose of medical care may be made available to a social worker for better understanding of a child care problem, and during the course of management be used for a totally different purpose, even a punitive one.

In this connection, too, I think again of the legal opinions on the relationship between the Local Authority elected councillors and employed social workers. I quote:

> once this [the relationship between Local Authority, Social Worker, clients of both] is understood it disposes of the professional objection to revealing confidential information to members of local authority on the basis that to do so would be a breach of a professional relationship. In fact such a dissemination of confidential information still keeps it within the boundary of professional relationship since this exists not only between social worker and client but also embraces the local authority itself. (extract from the opinion quoted above, p. 162)

It may be that elected councillors submit to a declared code of conduct and are liable to effective sanctions relating to it; but one would question the understanding and relative importance given to its observance by all elected councillors.

It is for the various reasons considered above that I believe that the medical profession would welcome wholeheartedly the broader establishment within the social work profession of a similar Code of Ethics stated and understood, with a central regulatory body to uphold its observance and which would have available real sanctions. This latter seems to be of prime importance. At the time of writing one can see the inefficacy of a professional body pronouncing on ethical standards in the absence of a structure for sanctions when one looks at the Press Council's efforts to control intrusion of privacy by the papers whose proprietors and editors can pursue whatever policy they wish regardless of the Press Council.

With such a wide range of training and qualifications pertaining to those involved in social work in the wider sense, difficulties also arise and some identification of a core of 'professional social work' might be necessary. We have seen also that work settings may give rise to complications which will have to be studied but it is certain that clarification of this whole matter would greatly enable interprofessional co-operation and may be crucial to allow the professional social worker to pursue the calling fully and effectively.

Notes

Chapter 1   What's the point of a Code of Ethics for Social Work?

1 If it still seems strange that what those in the paid occupation get up to might be *very* distant from the activities which are a means to the ends valued, and necessary if what they do is to be correctly called 'social work' at all, consider other cases. Is a policeman who does not aim to protect life and property a policeman? Is a doctor unconcerned to promote health a doctor? Each may, of course, have a job with the name in question, and so in that sense *be* a policeman or whatever, but at the same time each is *not* a policeman or whatever if not aiming at the relevant objectives, but engaged in other activities.

2 I choose 'rational' over alternatives such as 'sensitive' or 'effective' because it suggests that the measure is the capacity to argue for and justify one's practice. In my view, that social work has been done well is a matter demonstrated by exposing a line of thought, appropriately utilising what was known, reasonably believed, or a more plausible conjecture than alternatives. What must be demonstrated is that your actions were reasonably supposed to be the best available means to social work's purpose in this case. This is not to deny that sensitivity is an important ingredient in good social work, but even here the things we must be sensitive to are the indications which will contribute to social work of the kind I have called 'rational'. Again, I do not ignore effectiveness: rational activity is necessarily the best bet if we wish to be effective, even if the best laid plans of mice and men sometimes lead to traps.

3 Given that professional activity, I suggest, presupposes a relationship between the professional and a client in which that client has an acknowledged moral status, and that those granted special rights must acknowledge both general and special obligations if their unequal power is to be justified.

4 Strictly, they are 'members of the social work profession thus conceived', for alternative conceptions are available. It is not clear how we are to

decide when conceptions are sufficiently similar for us to describe holders, committed to their different implicit codes of practice, as members of *the same* profession, and I shall not pursue the point here. It is the same difficulty as theologians' struggle with distinguishing a sect from a different religion.

5 If we follow Barry (1964) and take the view that a policy promoting the interests of members of a profession is one that increases their opportunities to get what they want, whatever that may be, we leave logical space for such a policy not to be self-interested. What they want may be better provision for their clients.

Chapter 4   Responsibility in social work

1 A number of philosophers have argued that we are responsible (in a causal sense) for things that we could have prevented and yet did not prevent, as well as for those which we bring about directly. An extreme version of this position is adopted in Harris (1980).

2 Frequent reference to the importance of accepting responsibility for oneself is made in the writings and practice of humanistic psychologists, particularly those of Fritz Perls and other Gestalt therapists. In an interesting article, Rudestam advocates that clients be invited to change their linguistic habits. He argues that experiential and behavioural changes result from such modifications (Rudestam, 1978).

Chapter 6   Social work, professional social workers and the Code of Ethics

1 The compulsory admission procedure outlined here is the proposed procedure under the Mental Health (Amendment) Scotland Bill (Clause 13 amending Section 32 of the Principal Act 1960). This disengagement by the social worker from the case ought to happen less frequently under the requirements of this new Section 32A under sub-section 5 paragraphs A and B where the Local Authority has a new duty to provide a report on the patient. Furthermore, the question posed earlier concerning the practical applicability of the broad declarations of rights can be answered here. The right of appeal to the Sheriff (in Scotland) in the case of compulsory detention has now been included within the new Amendment Bill as a result of the 1960 Mental Health Act (Scotland) being in contravention of Article 5 (4) of the European Convention on Human Rights. However, under present practice (Section 31–7 days, 1960 Act) disengagement is relatively common and social work involvement in emergency admissions is low. Consent of next-of-kin or

of a mental health officer was absent in 61 per cent of cases admitted from outside hospital and in 83 per cent of cases within hospital in a study conducted over eight months on forty-eight subjects in Glasgow psychiatric hospitals (Gallacher *et al.*, 1983, pp. 4–13). In the development of this case illustration I revert to the existing statute Section 31 for clarity in the discussion of the social work task.

2 The list could include:

(a) Functions in the admission procedure: attempting to persuade the client to accept admission, perhaps voluntarily; offering comfort and support to the client who may be emotionally distressed; helping to avoid any damaging aspects of the experience of compulsory admission; assisting in transport arrangements; discussing aspects of the situation with the General Practitioner; exploring all alternative forms of care, e.g. availability of 'crisis' counselling; locating the next-of-kin and clarifying their possible assistance.

(b) Contribution to multi-disciplinary team and linkage between hospital and community.

(c) Discharge planning and the provision of after-care services.

(d) Self-help group membership.

3 'The Patient's Charter' therefore supports the right of each patient to the following:

(a) A reasonable standard of care and treatment.

(b) Privacy in such matters as dressing, toileting and handling of personal information.

(c) Dignity and respect as shown, for example, by courteous treatment, the use of appropriate names and help with regard to dress.

(d) Information concerning such things as treatment and its effects, hospital routine and activities.

(e) Freedom of decision, for example, to accept or reject treatment and also to seek a second opinion.

(f) Consideration of their views and wishes.

(g) The right to comment or complain about any aspect of the hospital service.

(h) Protection against physical or mental abuse.

Guide to further reading

The introduction and each chapter in this volume give abbreviated references to sources of further discussion of particular points arising. The references appear in full in the bibliography. A number of other sources may prove useful. Beginners might work through Raymond Plant's *Social and Moral Theory in Casework* (London, Routledge & Kegan Paul, 1970), Neil Leighton, Richard Stalley and David Watson's *Rights and Responsibilities* (London, Heinemann, 1980), Michael D. Bayles's *Professional Ethics* (Belmont, Wadsworth, 1981), or Noel Timms's *Social Work Values: An Enquiry* (London, Routledge & Kegan Paul, 1983).

As confidence grows, the following journals will prove a source of relevant discussion in some of their issues: *Journal of Applied Philosophy*, published by Carfax, and *Philosophy and Public Affairs*, published by Princeton University Press. Finally, books in the *International Library of Welfare and Philosophy* published by Routledge & Kegan Paul are also worth working through.

Bibliography

Aiken, H. D. (1956), *The Age of Ideology*, New York, Mentor Books.

Aiken, H. D. (1958), 'Morality and Ideology', in R. T. de George (ed.), *Ethics and Society*, London, Routledge & Kegan Paul.

Ainsworth, F. and Fulcher, L. (eds), (1981), *Group Care for Children: Concept and Issues*, London, Tavistock.

Arnold, M. (1970), *Selected Prose*, Harmondsworth, Penguin.

Assiglioni, R. (1974), *The Act of Will*, London, Wildwood House.

Association of Directors of Social Services (1982), *The Role and Tasks of Social Workers*, London, ADSS.

Barclay, P. (1982), *Social Workers, Their Role and Tasks*, the report of a Working Party set up by the National Institute for Social Work, chaired by Mr Peter M. Barclay, London, Bedford Square Press.

Barry, B. (1964), 'The public interest', *Proceedings of the Aristotelian Society*, supp, vol. 38, pp. 1–18, reprinted in A. Quinton (ed.), *Political Philosophy*, Oxford University Press, 1967.

Barry, B. (1965), *Political Argument*, London, Routledge & Kegan Paul.

BASW (1975a), *A Code of Ethics for Social Work*, adopted by the British Association of Social Workers, Birmingham, British Association of Social Workers.

BASW (1975b), 'Children at risk – BASW Code of Practice', *Social Work in Child Care*, Birmingham, British Association of Social Workers.

BASW/RCA (1976), *The Keyworker Concept*, Birmingham, British Association of Social Workers.

BASW (1980), *Clients are Fellow Citizens*, Birmingham, British Association of Social Workers.

BASW (1982), *Guidelines on Social Work with Severely Handicapped Infants*, Birmingham, British Association of Social Workers.

BASW (1983a), *Effective and Ethical Recording*, Birmingham, British Association of Social Workers.

BASW (1983b), *Social Workers and Employers: Policy and Guidance for Social Workers about Relationships with Employing Agencies*, Birmingham, British Association of Social Workers.

BASW (1983c), *Children in Care: Evidence to the House of Commons Social Services Committee Inquiry*, Birmingham, British Association of Social Workers.

BASW (1983d), *Determining and Regulating Standards of Conduct*, Birmingham, British Association of Social Workers.

Bell, M. (1961), *The Story of Hospital Almoners*, London, Faber & Faber.

Benn, S. I. and Peters, R. S. (1959), *Social Principles and the Democratic State*, London, Allen & Unwin.

Berridge, D. (1982) 'Developments in residential child care: children's homes in the 1980's', in *Managing to Care*, London, Residential Care Association.

Biestek, F. (1961), *The Casework Relationship*, London, Allen & Unwin.

Bradshaw, J. (1972), 'The concept of social need', *New Society*, 30 March.

Burchhardt, H. (1971), 'Zur Ausbildung von Sozialpädagogen in Fachschulen und Fachhochschulen unter besonderer Berucksichtigung der Ausbildung am Sozialpädagogischen Institut in Hamburg', in *Internationale Gesellschaft Für Heimerziehung*, Frankfurt-am-Main, IGH.

Campbell, T, D, (1978), 'Discretionary rights', in Timms and Watson (eds) (1978).

Capra, F. (1976), *The Tao of Physics*, London, Fontana.

CCETSW (1973), *Residential Work is Part of Social Work*, Discussion Paper 3, London, Central Council for Education and Training in Social Work.

CCETSW (1976), *Values in Social Work*, Discussion Paper 13, London, Central Council for Education and Training in Social Work.

Chamberlain, J. (1981), *On our own*, New York, McGraw Hill.

Checkland, P. B. (1981), *Systems Thinking, Systems Practice*, Chichester, Wiley.

Clark, D. (1974), *Social Therapy in Psychiatry*, Harmondsworth, Penguin.

Clayton, S. (1983), 'Social need revisited', *Journal of Social Policy*, 12,2.

Council of Europe (1982), *The European Convention on Human Rights*, Strasbourg, Council of Europe.

Culyer, A. J., Lavers, R. J. and Williams, A. (1972), 'Health indicators', in A. Shonfield and S. Shaw (eds), *Social Indicators and Social Policy*, London, Heinemann.

Dahrendorf, R. (1982), *On Britain*, London, British Broadcasting Corporation Publications.

Davis, A. (1981), *The Residential Solution: State Alternatives to Family Care*, London, Tavistock.

Downie, R. S. (1971), *Roles and Values*, London, Methuen.

Downie, R. S. and Telfer, E. (1980) *Caring and Curing*, London, Methuen.

Downie, R. S. and Telfer, E. (1969), *Respect for Persons*, London, Allen & Unwin.

Dowrick, C. (1983), 'Strange meeting: marxism and psychoanalysis and social work', *British Journal of Social Work*, 13, 1.

Dworkin, R. (1978), *Taking Rights Seriously*, London, Duckworth.

Essex County Council (1981), The Malcolm Page Inquiry Report.

Feinberg, J. (1973) *Social Philosophy*, Englewood Cliffs, New Jersey, Prentice-Hall.

Fromm, E. (1961), 'Marx's concept of man', in T. Bottomore (ed.), *Marx's Economic and Philosophical Manuscripts*, New York, Frederick Ungar.

Fromm, E. (1979), *To Have or To Be*, New York, Sphere Books.

Gallacher, J., Masterton, G. and Timbury, G. C. (1983), 'Section 31 (the Emergency Recommendation) – its use in a Glasgow psychiatric hospital', *Health Bulletin*, 4, 1.

Goldstein, H. (1983), 'Integration of theory and practice in social work education from a humanistic perspective', unpublished paper.

Halmos, P. (1978), *The Personal and the Political*, London, Hutchinson.

Harris, J. (1980), *Violence and Responsibility*, London, Routledge & Kegan Paul.

Hart, H. L. A. (1965), *Punishment and Responsibility*, Oxford University Press.

Hart, H. L. A. (1967), 'Are there any natural rights?', reprinted in A. Quinton (ed.), *Political Philosophy*, Oxford University Press.

Harvey, A. (1972), 'Publicity backlash', *New Society*, 12 October.

HMSO (1975), *Better Services for the Mentally Ill*, Cmnd. 6233, London, HMSO.

Hodges, H. A. (1944), *William Dilthey: An Introduction*, London, Routledge & Kegan Paul.

Hudson, J. R. (1975), 'Admission to care', *Social Work Today*, 6, 2.

Hudson, J. R. (1981a), 'Involving the family in sharing the caring', *Social Work Today*, 12, 28.

Hudson, J. R. (1981b), 'Probation hostels: wardens, regimes and residents', *Probation Journal*, 28, 1.

Hudson, J. R. (1981c), 'Every home should have a value system', *Social Work Today*, 12, 35.

Hudson, J. R. (1981d), 'A staff to support your value system', *Social Work Today*, 12, 43.

Illich, I. (1975), *Medical Nemesis*, London, Marion Boyars.

Jones, B. (1975), 'The rise and fall of local authority family casework in Great Britain', *International Social Work*, 18, 1.

Jones, K., Brown, J. and Bradshaw, J. (1978), *Issues in Social Policy*, London, Routledge & Kegan Paul.

Jordan, B. (1979), *Helping in Social Work*, London, Routledge & Kegan Paul.

King's Fund (1982), *Professionals and Volunteers: Partners or Rivals?*,

London, King's Fund Centre.

Klein, R. (1978), 'Normansfield: vacuum of management in the NHS, *British Medical Journal*, 23–30 December.

Lait, J. (1983), Letter to the *Daily Telegraph*, 11 January.

Lamb, M. (1981) (ed.), *The Role of the Father in Child Development*, Chichester, Wiley, 2nd edn.

Lao Tzu (1963), *Tao Te Ching*, Harmondsworth, Penguin.

Lewis, C. S. (1943), *The Abolition of Man*, London, Collins.

Lewis, R. and Maude, A. (1952), *Professional People*, London, Phoenix House.

Link: GAMH (1979), *Constitution of LINK: GAMH*, Glasgow, Glasgow Association for Mental Health.

McKinlay, J. (1973), 'On the professional regulation of change', in P. Halmos (ed.), *Professionalisation and Social Change, Sociological Review Monograph 20*, University of Keele Press.

McLachlan, G. and McKeon, T. (1971) (eds), *Medical History and Medical Care*, Oxford University Press.

Marshall, M. (1983), *Social Work Skills with the Elderly*, London, Macmillan.

Medawar, P. (1982), *Pluto's Republic*, Oxford University Press.

Mental Health Act (Scotland) 1960, ch. 61, London, HMSO.

Mental Health (Amendment) (Scotland) Bill 1981, HL, London, HMSO.

MIND (1980), *Manifestoes for Action*, London, MIND.

Morgan, P. (1983), 'The care racket', *Daily Telegraph*, 7 and 10 January.

Murdoch, I. (1970), *The Sovereignty of Good*, London, Routledge & Kegan Paul.

Newman, J. H. (1947), *The Idea of a University*, London, Longmans Green.

Nielsen, K. (1976), 'Alienation and self-realisation', in N. Timms and D. Watson (eds), *Talking About Welfare*, London, Routledge & Kegan Paul.

Parker, R. (1981), 'Tending and social policy', in E. M. Goldberg and S. Hatch (eds), *A New Look at the Personal Social Services*, London, Policy Studies Institute.

Plant, R., Lesser, H. and Taylor-Gooby, P. (1980), *Political Philosophy and Social Welfare*, London, Routledge & Kegan Paul.

Pragnell, C. (1983), 'C.S.S.: alive and well', *Social Work Today*, 18 January.

Rees, S. (1978), *Social Work Face to Face*, London, Edward Arnold.

Rowbottom, R., Billis, D. and Hey, A. (1974), *Social Services Departments: Developing Patterns of Work and Organisation*, London, Heinemann.

Rudestam, K. E. (1978), 'Semantics and psychotherapy', *Psychotherapy: Theory, Research and Practice*, 15, 2.

Sainsbury, E., Nixon, S. and Phillips, D. (1982), *Social Work in Focus*, London, Routledge & Kegan Paul.

Sartre, J. P. (1957), *Being and Nothingness*, London, Methuen.

Scarman, Lord (1974), *English Law, The New Dimension*, London, Stevens & Sons.

Scheff, T. (1966), *Being Mentally Ill: a Sociological Theory*, Chicago, Aldine Press.

Sheldon, B. (1978), 'Social influences: social work's missing link', in R. Olsen (ed.), *The Unitary Model*, Birmingham, BASW.

Singer, P. (1973), *Democracy and Disobedience*, London, Clarendon Press.

Smith, G. (1980), *Social Need*, London, Routledge & Kegan Paul.

Strawson, P. F. (1968), 'Freedom and resentment', in P. F. Strawson (ed.), *Studies in the Philosophy of Thought and Action*, London, Oxford University Press.

Timms, N. (1980) (ed.), *Social Welfare: Why and How?*, London, Routledge & Kegan Paul.

Timms, N. and Timms R. (1982), *A Dictionary of Social Welfare*, London, Routledge & Kegan Paul.

Timms, N. and Watson, D. (1978) (eds), *Philosophy in Social Work*, London, Routledge & Kegan Paul.

United Nations (1978), *The International Bill of Human Rights*, New York, UN.

de Vries, M. J. (1981), *The Redemption of the Intangible in Medicine*, *Psychosynthesis Monograph*, London, Institute of Psychosynthesis.

Wallace, G. and Walker, A. D. M. (1970) (eds), *The Definition of Morality*, London, Methuen.

Walton, R. (1978), 'Continuity and support for children in homes', *Social Work Today*, 9, 40.

Ward, L. (1977), 'Clarifying the residential social work task', *Social Work Today*, 9, 2.

Watson, D. (1978), 'Social services in a nutshell', in Timms and Watson (eds) (1978).

Watson, D. (1981), 'Discretion, moral judgment and integration', in M. Adler and S. Asquith (eds), *Discretion and Welfare*, London, Heinemann.

Watzlawick, P., Beavin, J. H. and Jackson, D. D. (1967), *Pragmatics of Human Communication*, New York, Norton.

Weil, S. (1962), *Selected Essays*, London, Oxford University Press.

Wilding, P. (1982a), *Professional Power and Social Welfare*, London, Routledge & Kegan Paul.

Wilding, P. (1982b), 'Partners with professionals', unpublished talk.

Wilkes, R. (1981), *Social Work with Underprivileged Groups*, London, Tavistock.

Williams, J. (1973), Presidential Address, *Residential Social Work*, 13, 11.
Winch, P. (1958), *The Idea of a Social Science*, London, Routledge & Kegan Paul.
Wolins, M. (1974), *Successful Group Care*, London, Aldine.
Younghusband, E. (1959), 'Report' of Working Party on Social Workers in the Local Authority Health and Welfare Services, Ministry of Health, Department of Health for Scotland, London, HMSO.

Index